TEAM CHURCH

Big-League Teamwork to Strengthen the Local Church

Gentry Sutton

GAZELLE
P R E S S

Team Church
by Gentry Sutton
Copyright ©2006 by Gentry Sutton

ISBN 1-58169-231-5
For Worldwide Distribution
Printed in the U.S.A.

Gazelle Press
P.O. Box 191540 • Mobile, AL 36619
800-367-8203

Table of Contents

DEDICATION

For Brooke, Isaac, Ian,
and Ireland, my favorite team

ACKNOWLEDGMENTS

I would like to thank the following people:

Hadley Hicks, Greg Stewart, and Jeremy Rogers for helping me see Christ on the baseball diamond; Keith Carroll for his literary suggestions and for allowing his talent and vision to be used by God; all my former baseball coaches, each of whom taught me something different and valuable.

I would also like to thank my parents and brothers for a lifetime of support.

To my three wonderful children I owe a special debt of gratitude. Their patience with me as I worked on this book was truly remarkable. They are remarkable, and they inspire me anew each day.

My lovely wife, Brooke, also deserves a great deal of credit. She is the most supportive soul I have ever met. She brings joy to my heart and is truly my better half.

G.S.
Pennsylvania
October 2006

INTRODUCTION

Seeing one person combine his or her abilities with another person's to reach a common goal has always inspired me. The process is called teamwork, and it's a fundamental aspect of God's will for humankind.

Everyone knows that teamwork is an essential part of a successful existence, yet many people approach the idea of working together with reluctance. After all, the very concept of teamwork exists in opposition to our fallen nature; to be effective members of a team, we must abandon selfish notions and think more about the greater good.

But there is also something within all of us that makes us want to be team members and experience the joy that comes from productive team endeavors. That's because, although we are fallen beings, we were created in God's image, and in the very image of God, expressed in the Holy Trinity and throughout His Word, are examples of teamwork. Therefore, teamwork is a significant part of God's design for the human experience. It is a gift He gave humanity at the beginning of time. And as a divinely given gift, we should incorporate it into our lives deliberately and often.

Throughout the Bible, there are inspiring and exemplary stories involving team accomplishments. The future King David escaped from Saul because of Jonathan's help. Jesus organized one of the greatest teams in history—the 12 apostles. Moses did not work alone; Aaron was almost always by his side. And teamwork is even reflected in the story of creation. According to Genesis 2:15, *"The Lord God took the man and put him in the Garden of Eden to work it and take care of it."* In verse 18, we find that God made a *helper* for Adam. Adam and Eve were created, in part, to work together.

But God has given us more than just stories about

people successfully working together. He has also given us a blueprint for teamwork, and it is found in 1 Corinthians 12:4-31, which is printed in full at the back of this book. In verses 8 through 10 of this passage, we read about eight different manifestations of the Holy Spirit: knowledge, wisdom, faith, miraculous powers, prophecy, discernment, messages in tongues, and the interpretation of tongues. Paul wrote that all of these manifestations were *"given for the common good"* (v. 7). Toward the end of the passage, Paul listed five additional ways to serve the greater good of Christ's body: apostleship, teaching, healing, helping others, and administrating. Many people refer to 1 Corinthians 12 as the spiritual gifts chapter, but it's really about more than just gifts. The majority of the passage deals with people using their gifts as a team. At its heart, the passage is about teamwork.

To illustrate the nature and importance of teamwork within Christ's body on earth, the Apostle Paul used the human body as a model. He compared spiritual gifts to various parts of the body, pointing out how each body part works in tandem with other parts. And Paul could not have chosen a better way to illustrate true teamwork. What do we know more intimately than our bodies? What is more complex? What is more essential to our survival than the proper maintenance and workings of our earthly bodies? Indeed, intimate, complex, and essential accurately describe the type of teamwork God calls his children to demonstrate.

Paul wrote that *"to **each one** the manifestation of the Spirit is given for the common good"* (1 Corinthians 12:7 emphasis added). What a wonderful promise! Everyone has something to contribute! And Paul's allusion to the human body, in conjunction with the fact that we are given gifts for the common good, teaches us that we are all in it together.

In the narrative that follows, I have used 1 Corinthians

12:4-31, in which Paul mentioned a number of spiritual gifts, as the foundation for a fictional story. With this passage as my model, I have composed a tale about the importance of baseball players using their individual gifts for the greater good of the team. As with athletes in other sports, baseball players must use their individual abilities to serve the greater good of the club. Players have different talents that must be used cooperatively for the team to be victorious. Sometimes the integration of players' abilities and responsibilities can be difficult and complicated. However, the players in this story are able to successfully fuse their various talents because they have an intimate knowledge of themselves, their gifts, their teammates, their teammates' gifts, and the game itself. In fact, in order to win the contest, it is essential that the players successfully combine their various talents—at times, in complex ways.

But the players are only part of the organization. At the professional level, an entire host of gifted people is necessary to keep things running smoothly. When we think of successful sports organizations, we usually think only of star power—and perhaps exemplary teamwork as it relates to the players. Imagine, however, a baseball team that has a terrible coaching staff, an unfair owner, a ground crew that never does its job properly, and vendors who have a way of putting spectators in bad moods. Chances are that the players in such an organization would not be successful. Everyone involved with a team is important to its success.

As a passionate baseball fan, I hope this story fosters a new appreciation for the game. Most important, though, it should remind readers of the need for all of us to use the gifts God has given us and to behave as a team when using them. Teamwork is not only about selflessly contributing our talents to a group endeavor but also about working in harmony with the other members of the group.

In the big picture of life, baseball is only a game. God's plan for His people, however, is not a game. A detailed look at the importance of teamwork in a sport should cause us to approach teamwork for God with new purpose. That is, if teamwork is important to the players in a game, then it should be a fundamental part of our lives as members of Christ's Church.

PREFACE

A NOTE BEFORE READING FURTHER

This book is based on 1 Corinthians 12, in which the Apostle Paul mentioned a number of spiritual gifts. Differing theological approaches to this passage have caused a great deal of controversy and confusion about its meaning. Even though the Apostle Paul wrote about spiritual gifts in the context of unity, disagreement and perhaps misunderstanding about certain gifts have been among the leading causes of divisiveness and dissension in the Body of Christ. I do not claim to have all the answers to the questions about spiritual gifts. This book is *not* a definitive work on the gifts of the Holy Spirit.

Paul told the Corinthians to be certain they used their spirituals gifts to build up (edify) the church (1 Corinthians 14:12). As you read the following chapters, you will see that the word "edify" carries two meanings in Scripture. As the early Christians used their gifts, they helped to build up the church by growing it larger in number. By using their gifts, they helped bring people to a saving belief in Jesus Christ. The early disciples also edified the church by helping to build the strength of individual believers. In both senses, the church was edified by the use of the various gifts of the first-century Christians.

When Paul used the human body as an illustration of the importance of Christians using their spiritual gifts in concert, he was emphasizing teamwork. Teamwork is the focus of this book.

In each chapter, you will find biblical evidence that certain qualities of different people edified the Body of Christ. I make the distinction between qualities and gifts for a reason. In most cases, I cannot be certain that the gift-related things people did to build up the church were necessarily the result of spiritual gifts, as many Christians believe them to be. For example, one of the gifts Paul mentioned in 1 Corinthians 12 was faith. In chapter six of this book, I write about how the faith of the Thessalonians edified the Body of Christ, but Scripture does not indicate that their faith was a spiritual gift. Some believers make a distinction between the gift of faith and the faith that we are all called to demonstrate, and some believers do not. Nevertheless, the nature of the language tells me that the basic essence of faith will be the same whether it is a gift or not.

While this book is not a definitive work on spiritual gifts, it is a reminder that the most important lessons of 1 Corinthians 12 have nothing to do with understanding the complexities of each gift. I believe the imperative lessons of this beautiful chapter are more about action and unity.

All of God's people have a responsibility to use their individual gifts to serve the greater good, and they should do so in harmony. 1 Corinthians 12 is a model illustration of what God intended teamwork to look like. As Paul pointed out, by using the example of the human body, teamwork in the Body of Christ involves Christians working together efficiently and in unity. As Christians, we should use our various gifts and talents in the pursuit of goodness. As we do so, each person will be made better and more productive because of the other gifts and talents on the team. In short, teamwork in the Body of Christ is everyone's business, and it does not work properly unless we all use our God-given gifts in a spirit of cooperation, love, and service.

CHAPTER 1

Some Help Others

The home team is having one if its best seasons ever, and to many fans and sportswriters the reason is obvious. Earlier in the year, the media dubbed them "The Diamond Family" because of their sparkling play and unusual unity on the field. It's apparent that every player knows and accepts his role, no matter how large or how small it is. Moreover, each player seems to understand that his own gifts and abilities work best in tandem with those of the other players. As a result, the team has been in first place since the second week of the season.

Not as obvious to fans and reporters is the fact that the players are not the only members of the organization who are unified. From top management down to the peanut and cotton candy vendors, it seems that everyone is on the same page. When Boss, the team's owner, purchased the franchise at the end of the previous season, he implemented radical ideas that changed the entire environment. Although some investors disagreed with his management style, Boss was convinced that a progressive approach to organizational unity would breed success. He lives by the golden rule, and so in his quest to foster harmony throughout the organization, he announced higher wages and health insurance for every employee. He also urged his people—from players and executives to ticket takers and stadium custodians—to gather periodically and share ideas for improvement. The employees meet biweekly in the stadium to hear a brief address from Boss and to voice their suggestions. Boss always praises each division of the franchise and takes every single idea seriously. Players have come to appreciate all the "little people" who make the organization a success.

From his upper-deck suite behind home plate, Boss panoramically peruses the stadium, and what he sees fills him with satisfaction. His organization reminds him of a well-oiled, complex machine. Everyone has a place, and each person appears comfortable performing his duties. The fans seem peaceful, the vendors and ushers are enjoying their work and their interaction with the people, and the players are eager to play. It does not escape Boss's notice that almost every fan in the stadium is smiling.

The organizational unity has indeed made for an enjoyable season for the fans. Not only are they relishing the club's success, they are also finding their time in the stands to be more pleasurable than ever before. Since all the workers in the park understand that they are an important part of the franchise and that they all contribute in different yet meaningful ways, the high morale in the organizational atmosphere is almost tangible. There are no rude popcorn vendors or pushy ushers in this stadium. Moreover, employees actually *offer* to help people whenever they can. Whether it's helping a child to get down a short flight of stairs in the box seats or offering to hold drinks as parents get their children seated, the vendors and ushers help make the atmosphere at this stadium one of generous service.

As enthused spectators begin to fill the seats for a

Sunday afternoon contest, the ground crew is working on the playing field with the orchestration of a small army. All the crew members are dressed alike, wearing pinstriped tee shirts with the home team's logo on the right sleeve. A hard morning rain has left behind a couple of puddles, one on the warning track in right field and another near the visiting team's bullpen. Luckily, the alert ground crew covered the entire infield with a giant tarpaulin the night before. It is an incredibly heavy mass of material, and it takes 12 men to roll the colossal canvas off the playing field, each member of the crew pulling his own weight. Seeing the perfectly dry earth beneath, however, makes the work worthwhile.

The removal of the tarp is the most difficult part of the ground crew's job, but the workers still have plenty to do. Once the tarp is out of the way, they break into smaller groups, each to perform different tasks. Some dry the mud on the warning track so outfielders will not slip and fall. Others pump water from each puddle. Still others sponge water from the grass in the outfield and foul territory, where the tarp had not covered the ground.

As the members of the ground crew perform their individual duties, Bullpen Catcher rises from his seat and puts on his mitt. Starting Pitcher, to the applause of excited fans in the outfield's "cheap seats," is approaching the bullpen to begin his pregame warm-up. Bullpen Catcher seldom plays in actual games, and his job of getting pitchers ready is often a thankless one. But he doesn't care. He knows that his team is well on its way to a championship, and he is happy to do his part to help.

Just as Bullpen Catcher helps Starting Pitcher warm up, other nonstarting players begin to help the fielders in the starting lineup to prepare for the game. For example, Utility, who can play almost any position on the field but sees only three or four innings of action per week, is helping Center Field stretch his arms and legs. Southpaw, a left-handed pitcher who started the day before and therefore has the day off, is busy in the bullpen preparing the pitching charts. The charts are especially important in today's game because Starting Pitcher has a sensitive arm. Trainer, the team's medical professional, has suggested that the hurler's activity be monitored carefully.

Another nonstarter, Rookie, is also helping some of the players prepare for the game. Only recently called up to the major-league level, Rookie has quickly found favor with his teammates. Each day he demonstrates a genuine team attitude, always asking various starters if he can do anything for them. Whether it is helping another player stretch, hitting grounders to infielders, or just playing catch with one of the more experienced players, as he is today, Rookie does whatever he can. And his willing attitude has not gone unnoticed by Skipper, the team's manager. Though he still has a lot to learn, the newcomer has been invited to join the team because of his exceptional speed. Skipper would love to reward the youngster for his attitude by giving him a chance to show off that speed in a game as soon as possible.

In the dugout, Coach, who is Skipper's right-hand man, is studying the visiting team's lineup card and making notes. Trainer is stocking the dugout's medicine corner with ice packs, pain relievers, and other first-aid items.

As different players prepare in their own ways and as more fans file through the gates, the ground crew continues to create a work of art on the diamond. Within moments it is difficult to tell that only a few hours earlier most of the turf was soaked with rain. In a period of five minutes, 12 men have done the work of 20 men.

The game has not even started, but a number of players

and other personnel have already contributed meaningfully to the day's contest. Without the many people who are willing to do thankless jobs, the home team might not be having the wonderful season it is having.

———

I grew up playing baseball in a small western Oklahoma town. Given its rural makeup and down-home tradition, few people ever left the area, and because of its struggling economy, even fewer people moved in; consequently, I played with the same group of teammates from the age of 7 to the age of 18. And because we played together for so long, we developed some great on-the-field chemistry—enough to win us one state title and twice finish as state runners-up when we were in high school.

Our team chemistry carried us a long way, and we had a little talent, too. But as I look back on those years, I realize that my teammates and I were only part of the winning equation. We had lots of help from a lot of other people. In fact, my hometown is one of the most baseball-friendly communities in the state of Oklahoma.

The year we won the state title, we played the championship game in front of approximately 500 people—a nice sized crowd for a couple of high schools that had some 250 students combined. I remember being proud that almost 400 of those spectators were there to support my team. The community had always supported my teammates and me, even when we were young children. But it didn't show its support just by its presence at games. My team never wanted for anything. We always had the best equipment and anything else we needed. Community members helped us in any way they could.

Thanks in large part to the community, we also had one

of the nicest baseball diamonds in the entire state. Many generous parents made sure that we had the best turf, dirt, sprinkler system, batting cages, and other luxuries that money could buy.

It's one thing to help from one's pocketbook, but what always inspired me the most were the fathers who would lend their time to maintain the diamond, repairing it after torrential downpours or spending entire days working on the field between seasons. Along with our beautiful diamond, we also had one of the greatest ground crews in the state—an all-volunteer crew. I don't think my high school team would have enjoyed its great success had it not been for parents and other community members who were willing to help us reach our goals.

Like the ground crew at a baseball game, or a bullpen catcher, or a nonstarting infielder who selflessly gives his time to help the "stars" be the best they can be, the early church had many helpers, people who served out of the spotlight but whose work was important, nonetheless. Luke, the author of Acts, wrote about a helper named Apollos. In Achaia, this passionate man *"was a great help to those who by grace had believed. For he vigorously refuted the Jews in public debate, proving from the Scriptures that Jesus was the Christ"* (Acts 18:27-28).

The Apostle Paul also made mention of helpers. For instance, he wrote to the Romans:

> *I commend to you our sister Phoebe, a servant of the church in Cenchrea. I ask you to receive her in the Lord in a way worthy of the saints and to give her any help she may need from you, for she has been a great help to many people, including me* (Romans 16:1-2).

Some Help Others

Later in the chapter we learn that someone helped Paul
with the actual transcription of his letter to the Romans.
Romans 16:22 reads, "*I, Tertius, who wrote down this
letter, greet you in the Lord.*"
Paul mentioned other helpers, too. In 2 Timothy he
wrote, "*Get Mark and bring him with you, because he is
helpful to me in my ministry*" (4:11). He mentioned fellow
helpers or workers on many occasions. While Paul was one
of the visible leaders of the early church, he was also aware
that much went on behind the scenes. Believers gathered
for worship in homes, not in large buildings with steeples,
and they usually dined together. Obviously, many people
had to help out in a variety of ways. Meals had to be prepared, and homes had to be arranged to accommodate large
gatherings. It must have been a wonderful sight to see so
many people selflessly doing what it took to keep the church
functioning.

CHAPTER 2

Some Are Apostles

The first pitch of the game is only moments away. Most of the fans are now in their seats, and the ground crew is removing the last of its equipment from the diamond. Starting Pitcher has finished warming up in the bullpen and has made his way to the cooler for one last drink before taking the field.

Seated directly above the home team's dugout are an excited little boy and his father. The father, named Lost, is at the park only at his son's request, for Lost has developed an aversion to baseball since childhood. Because he had a bad youth-league experience as a child and because he watches too much television, Lost's perception of the game is very negative. Mostly due to the unfavorable media attention that the game has received recently, Lost has come to believe that all professional players are greedy individuals who threaten to strike every other year and who charge outrageous sums of money just to sign autographs. When at home, Lost often discourages his son's love of baseball and the boy's admiration of his favorite player, Shortstop, who is one of the fans' favorites.

Seated directly to Lost's right is a man named Scout.

Scout travels the country seeking new talent for the home team. He's been doing the same job for years and has enjoyed every day of it. He loves the game, he loves meeting new people, and he loves being an ambassador for baseball everywhere he goes. He spends his days off at the park, cheering for his favorite group of players.

As the umpires, managers, and coaches gather at home plate to discuss the ground rules, Scout strikes up a conversation with Lost. "Nice day for a game," he says.

"Not bad," Lost replies, indifference evident in his tone.

"Do you come to the park often?" Scout inquires.

"No. I don't even like baseball. I'm only here for my son. Shortstop is his hero."

"Well, you must be a dedicated father," Scout says cordially. "Why don't you like baseball?"

"Lots of reasons, I suppose. Mainly, I believe it's too much of a business and that too many 'stars' at the professional level are setting bad examples for our kids. I mean, these guys make enough money to have everything they want, yet it seems as if they always want more."

"Well, they're not all like that," Scout retorts. "There are still some extraordinarily nice guys playing baseball today. Sure, you see a few bad apples on the news now and then, but the news usually fails to report the brighter side of the game."

Surprised by Scout's frankness and sincerity, Lost sinks a little in his seat.

"Think about all the charity work that some of these guys do," Scout continues. "Baseball feeds and clothes thousands of children each year. Many of these players donate millions of dollars to charities and use their star power to raise money for a variety of good causes.

"The game of baseball also provides a way for thousands

of young men to go to college. Most college programs carry at least 20 players, which translates into a lot of scholarships nationwide. It's because of these scholarships that many young men meet their wives and achieve their career goals in all different types of businesses.

"And I can't think of a better game to foster such a variety of life skills—teamwork, camaraderie, imagination, hard work, individual responsibility. I would hate to live in a nation where children were deprived of the opportunity to play baseball."

Lost now feels foolish. Who is this man sitting next to him, this man who speaks so passionately about the game?

The child's eyes sparkle as they look at Scout. The stranger has made a good case against his father's dislike of the game.

When he sees the boy peer into the dugout, trying his best to catch an up-close glimpse of his favorite player, Scout is filled with compassion. He cranes his neck over the iron rail that separates the fans from the diamond and shouts into the dugout, "Hey, Shortstop, aren't you even going to say hello?"

Shortstop looks up from his seat on the dugout bench to see his old friend, Scout, the man who arranged his first professional contract many years before. The performer smiles as he climbs from the sunken structure to the rail.

The little boy's heart begins to pound in his chest—his favorite big-league player is walking directly toward him! As the child realizes that Shortstop and the stranger apparently know each other and will have a conversation in his presence, everything else in the world suddenly becomes unimportant.

"Shouldn't you be working?" Shortstop playfully asks Scout as the two old friends shake hands.

"Day off," Scout replies. "Besides, if I were working, I might find your replacement."

Shortstop laughs, and the two men begin to catch up on each other's lives. They discuss the weather, their families, the opposing team, and the charity work that Shortstop is doing for orphaned children.

As Lost pretends not to listen, his son watches Shortstop's every move. After a few moments, the boy can barely contain his excitement, and he peers up at Scout as if begging to be introduced to the man he has come to watch.

Using body language, Scout gives Shortstop a hint that the little boy is a big fan. The two men share the opinion that players, as well as the entire organization, should show appreciation and respect to fans.

Shortstop, known for being fan friendly, looks at the child and says, "Hello, young man. Ready to see a good game?"

"Yes," comes the boy's brief reply. He is too nervous to say more.

"I see you've brought your glove. Hoping to catch a foul ball?"

"Yep!"

"Well, just in case you don't, let me see if I can find something in the dugout for you."

Shortstop then disappears down the dugout steps, reemerging a few moments later with a pearly white baseball that he has autographed in blue ink. He makes more small talk with the boy before finishing his conversation with Scout.

Lost subtly reaches for his program to read about the player; he is bewildered by the star's warmhearted dialogue with the child. Only a few moments earlier, Lost had expressed his sincere disdain for baseball, noting that players seem to be greedy individuals who care much about money and fame but little about their fans. Within minutes, one of the most popular players in the league was standing before him, unknowingly challenging much of what he had heard and read about the game at the professional level. Moreover, fate had seated him next to an outspoken ambassador for not only the home team but also the sport.

As Lost reads about Shortstop in the program, he feigns a lack of interest in Shortstop's conversation with Scout. In reality, he is listening intently. The scout and the shortstop are not the type of men whom he has come to associate with professional baseball. They have opened his eyes to a side of the game he did not know existed.

———

Like other sports, the game of baseball has certainly taken its knocks from the media during the past few years—much of the time, with good reason. At the professional level, there have been unfortunate player-coach arguments, violent player-fan and player-umpire incidents, greed-ridden player-owner skirmishes, and many troubling cases of steroid abuse. Sadly, overly competitive parents have caused problems in youth leagues, too. Almost all of these occurrences make the headlines, which influence many people's opinions about the game. However, stories about all the good that comes from baseball—the millions of dollars given to charities, wonderful character-building camps for young players, and thousands of college scholarships—are seldom reported.

When I transferred from a junior college to a Christian college as a young student-athlete, I experienced firsthand what it was like to be unfairly stereotyped. Although I played ball for a college that was known for its student body's love for Christ, some of my teammates did typical college-student things sometimes (and I certainly was no angel as an undergraduate). Many of the baseball players enjoyed sowing a few wild oats. Unfortunately, there are few secrets on a small, close-knit Christian college campus in the heart of Kansas, and a series of events helped the baseball team earn a less than desirable reputation within the college community. Poor academic performance and minimal scholastic effort by some players forced a few professors to be unforgiving of late papers and sporadic attendance. Other professors became less willing to cooperate with our hectic game and practice schedules. Furthermore, a few of the players' nighttime social habits affected many students' perception of the team as a whole. Some of the guys on the team were unfairly condemned as guilty by association of leading less than Christian lifestyles.

After news of certain events reached our coach, he understandably grew perturbed. I recall him telling my teammates and me that our team reputation was in the cellar and that it was our responsibility to change it. He challenged us to behave ourselves, both academically and socially, and to win back the trust of the campus community with our actions. In essence, he was telling us to go and be ambassadors for our baseball team.

In the story, Scout realizes how the game of baseball has been victimized by an imbalance of positive and negative publicity, and he uses his gift as an ambassador of the game (or an apostle) to counter the unfairness. The early church also faced negative publicity—from both Jews and Gentiles. Paul was certainly aware of Christianity's reputation, and he knew how to effectively address the problem. In his letter to the Ephesians, he wrote that he was an "ambassador" for the Gospel (6:20). Much as Scout and Shortstop challenge a

13

spectator's media-based assumptions by simply spreading goodwill, Paul understood that part of an apostle's job was to serve as an ambassador of the faith.

Scout exemplifies an apostle in another way, too: He understands the importance of boldness. He speaks boldly about the benefits of baseball, making no apologies for challenging a total stranger's erroneous beliefs. Similarly, the early church needed apostles who would challenge secular public opinion about Christianity. The New Testament contains many passages that refer to the apostles' boldness of speech. For example, in the book of Acts, we learn that Paul, in Damascus, "*had preached fearlessly in the name of Jesus*" (9:27) and that he "*moved about freely in Jerusalem, speaking boldly in the name of the Lord*" (9:28). Indeed, in Acts 18:9-10, we learn that the Lord himself encouraged Paul to be bold: "*One night the Lord spoke to Paul in a vision: 'Do not be afraid; keep on speaking, do not be silent. For I am with you, and no one is going to attack and harm you, because I have many people in this city.'*"

The early apostles needed to be bold because the message of the gospel was unpopular. Part of the apostles' job was to convince unbelievers that Jesus is the promised Messiah, and this was definitely not the best way to make friends. Nevertheless, in Acts 19:8, we read that "*Paul entered the synagogue and spoke boldly there for three months, arguing persuasively about the kingdom of God.*" We learn from Acts 9:29 that he "*talked and debated with the Grecian Jews.*" And when Paul and Barnabas were in Iconium trying to persuade the Jews to accept Christ's message, they were also challenging popular thought. Although they did not convert everyone, they had much success:

At Iconium Paul and Barnabas went as usual into

the Jewish synagogue. There they spoke so effectively that a great number of Jews and Gentiles believed. But the Jews who refused to believe stirred up the Gentiles and poisoned their minds against the brothers. So Paul and Barnabas spent considerable time there, speaking boldly for the Lord, who confirmed the message of his grace by enabling them to do miraculous signs and wonders. The people of the city were divided; some sided with the Jews, others with the apostles (Acts 14:1-4 emphasis added).

When *"the Jews who refused to believe stirred up the Gentiles and poisoned their minds against the brothers,"* Paul and Barnabas did not become discouraged and complacent. Instead, they did the exact opposite. The word *so* in the above passage is emphasized for an important reason— it tells us there was cause and effect. It was precisely *because* of the Jews' disbelief and their poisoning of the Gentiles' minds that Paul and Barnabas stayed.

Because of their boldness, ambassadorship, and gift with rhetoric, the apostles were able to challenge public opinion about Christianity and bring many people to a belief in Jesus Christ. In short, Paul understood an important truth about the gift of apostleship: When apostles served as ambassadors and spoke boldly and "effectively," the church as a whole was strengthened and built up. Apostleship was a gift that benefited all of God's team.

CHAPTER 3

Some Speak in Tongues and Some Interpret

After Starting Pitcher delivers his final warm-up toss before the first inning of play, the home plate umpire pulls his mask over his face and shouts, "Play ball!" His order brings with it thunderous applause from the anxious fans.

Leadoff, the visiting team's first batter, confidently paces from the on-deck circle to the batter's box. He appears incredibly focused, determined to reach base as quickly as possible. He pays no attention to the thousands of fans cheering against him.

Catcher, comfortable but intense as he sits a little more than 60 feet away from the pitcher's plate, holds down one finger when Starting Pitcher takes his position. The pitcher knows that "one" is the signal for a fastball, and he nods, winds up, and throws the first pitch, a straight fastball that crosses the outside corner of home plate.

The fans cheer even louder at the umpire's declaration of "Strike!" but Leadoff appears unaffected by the noise. After a couple of practice swings, he confidently returns to the batter's box for the second pitch.

Catcher again drops a single finger, and Starting Pitcher

agrees to throw another fastball. Unfortunately, the hurler proves imperfect with what is only his second pitch of the game. Leadoff deems the fastball inviting and belts a line drive over the third baseman's head. The very first batter has ruined Starting Pitcher's chance at a no-hitter. There are no outs, and a runner is on first.

Leadoff is the fastest base runner in the league. He already holds the single-season record for stolen bases, and he is on a pace to outdo himself this year. As Second Batter steps up to home plate, the defense prepares itself for the likelihood that Leadoff will try to steal second.

Starting Pitcher does all he can to prevent Leadoff from advancing. Before he even delivers a pitch to the next batter, the hurler makes three consecutive throws to first base in an attempt to pick off the speedy runner. However, Leadoff dives safely back to the canvas bag during all three attempts.

When Starting Pitcher finally throws a pitch, Leadoff wastes no time using his speed. The determined runner ducks his head and races toward second base. The batter does not swing at the pitch, and Catcher receives the ball and makes a quick, accurate throw to second. But Leadoff is simply too fast. He slides safely into the bag and even pops to his feet before he is tagged. With no outs, there is now a runner on second.

Although the previous pitch was a strike and Second Batter is already behind in the count, the defense still faces a significant problem. Catcher must now be careful when he flashes his signs to Starting Pitcher, for the runner at second base is in a perfect position to steal the catcher's signals. If Leadoff learns what pitch will be thrown next, he will alert his teammate in the batter's box and cause even more problems for the home team. Luckily, Catcher and Starting

Pitcher have been in this position before, and they know just what to do. Starting Pitcher knows that when a runner is at second base, he is to interpret the fourth of a series of signs that Catcher flashes, not the first. This secret language between the pitcher and the catcher makes it much more difficult for a sneaky base runner to steal signs and share them with his teammate in the batter's box.

The secret language, however, is not exclusive to Catcher and Starting Pitcher—two other home-team players also understand the code. As Starting Pitcher positions himself on the pitcher's plate to throw the next pitch, Shortstop and Second Base fulfill a seemingly small responsibility of their jobs. When Catcher flashes his pitch signals, the two middle infielders study his fingers closely. Because of their view of Catcher, they are the only two players on the team, other than the pitcher, of course, who can see Catcher's signs entirely. The two middle infielders are thus interpreters for the entire team, and their interpretive duties can be important. When Starting Pitcher is going to throw a fastball, Shortstop and Second Base simply lean slightly to their left as they ready for the pitch. If the pitch will be off-speed, they lean to their right. This allows every member of the defense to know what pitch is coming. Right-handed hitters such as Second Batter have a tendency to hit off-speed pitches to left field, while they often hit fastballs to center field or right field. Although this isn't always the case, baseball is a game of percentages. Moreover, it is a game of inches, and a fielder who has a good idea of where the ball might be hit is a fielder who can make a big difference in a game.

As Second Batter awaits Starting Pitcher's next offering, Shortstop and Second Base both lean slightly to their left, indicating that Catcher has called for a fastball. After glancing at the base runner, Starting Pitcher delivers a pitch that speeds toward the outside part of the strike zone. Due to its fast velocity and its location, Second Batter connects with the ball on a plane that forces the ball down the first-base line.

First Base had heeded the middle infielders' forewarning and had moved one step closer to the foul line as the pitch neared the strike zone. Thanks to his knowledge of what pitch was being thrown, he had positioned himself to field a ball that ordinarily might have eluded his grasp. Diving acrobatically to his left, toward foul territory, he snags the well-hit line drive before the ball touches the ground.

Leadoff has no choice but to stay put. Now there is one out and a man on second base.

The fans applaud First Base's athleticism, but their enthusiasm wanes when Starting Pitcher walks Third Batter on four straight pitches. Although no one is aware of it, the hurler is already experiencing pain in his arm because of a nagging condition. The home team is now in its worst position of the game—one out, runners on first and second, Starting Pitcher with a troubled arm, and the best hitter in the visiting team's starting lineup stepping into the batter's box.

As Fourth Batter awaits his first pitch, Shortstop and Second Base once again interpret Catcher's signals. When they learn that the next pitch will be a curveball, they lean casually to their right, secretively alerting the defense to a probable play on the third-base side of the field.

Playing the percentages pays off again—in a big way. Starting Pitcher's curveball spins toward the center of the strike zone, and Fourth Batter cannot wait to swing as hard as he can. Because he swings early, the angle of the bat forces the ball down the third-base line.

Relying on the middle infielders' information, Third Base has moved slightly toward his bag, placing himself a step or two closer to the immediate play. As the well-hit ground ball bounds down the foul line, Third Base dives to his right, gloving it before it rolls into the outfield. He quickly rises to one knee and makes an amazing throw to Second Base, who then receives the ball, steps on his own bag, and throws to First Base for a double play.

The field umpires declare the runners out, and the stadium erupts with applause. The fielders congratulate each other on their teamwork, and Starting Pitcher jogs off the diamond and into the dugout, where he will spend a few minutes with Trainer. Luckily, the pitcher did not have to throw too many pitches during the first inning; however, the pain in his arm is already intensifying.

Though not one spectator is aware of it, Shortstop's and Second Base's sign interpretations have likely helped to prevent the other team from scoring. If First Base and Third Base had not been aware of what pitches were being thrown, they might not have made successful fielding plays.

As a young ballplayer, I played under one nationally recognized coach who emphasized the importance of good communication among the players on a ball diamond. Baseball players need to communicate with each other almost constantly, especially when they are on defense. But as the story illustrates, players don't always have the luxury of using direct speech, and when they do talk, what they say is not always what they mean.

For example, when I occasionally played shortstop, I was charged with the same task that the shortstop in the story is charged with: informing the rest of the defense what pitch was about to be thrown. I would do this in a couple of ways. Suppose our pitcher's name was John Doe. If he were about to throw a fastball, I might say, "Come on, John. Give us a strike." The fact that I used the pitcher's first name would tell the entire defense that a fastball was about to be thrown. If I said, "Throw it in there, Doe," the defense could expect a curveball, since I had used the pitcher's last name. Or I might pound my mitt to signal a fastball or lick my fingers to signal a curveball. Such details might seem trivial to the casual baseball fan, but a defense that knows what pitch is coming is a defense with an advantage. Knowing the velocity and intended location of a pitch helps a defensive player decide how to shift his body weight or know whether he should take a step in a certain direction. And one step can be the difference between victory and loss in baseball. As the defense's interpreter of the secret language between the pitcher and catcher, I was helping to strengthen the team as a whole.

The language of baseball signals illustrates two important points regarding what the Bible teaches about tongues and interpretations. Both signs in baseball and tongues and interpretations in the Bible are used for instruction and for the benefit of the entire body.

In America's pastime, even the simplest of motions are used as signs that communicate knowledge that is to be spread to the entire team. If the catcher thinks a curveball should be thrown, he will indicate as much by relaying a sign to the pitcher. This sends a message not only to the pitcher, but also to attentive shortstops and second basemen so that they can communicate the plan to the rest of the defense. Similarly, in the second chapter of Acts we learn that when the apostles were filled with the Holy Spirit and began to speak in tongues at Pentecost (v. 4), they spoke of "*the wonders of God"* in different languages so that all who were present could understand (v. 11). In short, the apostles were instructing the Jews in the ways of God. Paul emphasized the importance of the instructional element of tongues when he wrote to the Corinthians,

> *Now, brothers, if I come to you and speak in tongues, what good will I be to you, unless I bring you some revelation or knowledge or prophecy or word of instruction?* (1 Corinthians 14:6).

But like all gifts, tongues and interpretations were to be used for the benefit of the entire Body. When the middle infielders interpret the catcher's signals (tongues), they share the message with the entire team. As a result, the other players are much better prepared to defend their opponents' aggression.

Paul related this concept to the church when he wrote to the Corinthians:

> *Undoubtedly there are all sorts of languages in the world, yet none of them is without meaning. If then I do not grasp the meaning of what someone is saying, I am a foreigner to the speaker, and he is a foreigner to me. So it is with you. Since you are eager to have spiritual gifts, try to excel in the gifts that build up the church* (1 Corinthians 14:10-12).

The allusion to speaking in tongues is obvious enough in the example above, but what Paul wrote immediately after these verses added clarification to his point. In verse 13 he wrote, *"For this reason anyone who speaks in a tongue should pray that he may interpret what he says."* The "reason" to which Paul referred is contained in his previous statement. He wanted to make it clear that gifts were to build up the church. When messages spoken in tongues were interpreted, the entire group of believers was edified. If messages were not interpreted, only the speaker was edified. Paul made the point even more clear when he wrote:

When you come together, everyone has a hymn, or a word of instruction, a revelation, a tongue or an interpretation. All of these must be done for the strengthening of the entire church (1 Corinthians 14:26).

Paul was criticizing the Corinthian Christians for not conducting their worship services in an appropriate manner. We know from other parts of the letter that the lack of order resulted from divisions and selfishness among church members. Paul was emphasizing that gifts were not to be used to gain prestige or fulfill selfish needs. On the contrary, he reminded the Corinthians that gifts were to be used for the benefit of the entire church body.

CHAPTER 4

Some Have Knowledge

After an unproductive half-inning on offense, the home team gets off to a bad defensive start in the top of the second. Starting Pitcher has begun the inning by walking Fifth Batter and has, thus, broken one of the cardinal rules of baseball. Giving a "free ride" to the first batter of any inning is bad strategy, to say the least.

Because of the walk, the visiting team is now in a position to employ a number of different offensive tactics. First, Fifth Batter could attempt to steal second base. If successful, his team would be in an extremely advantageous position. Having a runner at second base with no outs drastically increases the likelihood of scoring.

A second possibility is that the visiting team could simply hope for a hit from the next batter. Even a single could move the runner from first base to third base.

A third option is that Sixth Batter could execute a sacrifice bunt in order to advance the runner. If a ball is bunted on the ground, the runner at first base will almost certainly reach second base because the defense will have a difficult time fielding such a slowly rolling ball and then throwing it to the center of the diamond in time to retire the runner.

The batter who actually bunts the ball, however, will likely be thrown out at first base; hence the term "sacrifice." The batter essentially sacrifices his turn at bat so that a runner can advance.

The situation of having a runner at first base with no outs often creates mental guesswork for coaches and managers on defense. Luckily, the home team has the best research and statistics department of any team in the league. Many hard-working employees, under the direction of upper-management individuals such as Boss, Skipper, and Coach, have compiled a database that is full of information about hundreds of players from different teams. The information does not always help to accurately predict outcomes, but it is valuable, nonetheless.

Before Skipper decides how best to arrange his defense, he needs to know what Sixth Batter normally does in such a situation. After blowing a large bubble with his chewing gum, he turns to Coach and asks, "What's the scouting report say?"

Coach, who always sits in the same corner of the dugout and keeps a small library of information at his disposal, flips through the pages of a giant notebook until he comes to the page containing information about Sixth Batter. "Good runner. Prefers to hit fastballs. Leads the team in sacrifice bunt attempts."

"Well," replies Skipper, "we should probably play for the bunt then."

"I agree," says Coach. "Here's something that has just been added to the report. The stats indicate that he has a strong tendency to pop up when trying to bunt inside fastballs."

"Interesting," Skipper says. "It would be nice if he would do that now."

After a few more words with Skipper about the defensive strategy, Coach climbs to the top of the dugout steps so that all of the infielders can see him. He gives signals that instruct his players to expect a bunt and rotate accordingly if the ball is indeed bunted. While using a separate set of signals, he also tells Catcher to call for inside fastballs from Starting Pitcher.

When the hurler once again takes his position on the pitcher's plate, Catcher does as instructed and calls for an inside fastball. The pitcher nods, sets, and delivers the pitch exactly as Catcher has asked for it.

Playing right to the home team's plan, Sixth Batter squares around to bunt, while Fifth Batter waits cautiously at first base, hoping to see the ball bounce off his teammate's bat in a downward trajectory. If it does, he will sprint toward second base as fast as he can.

Fortunately for the home team, the ball does not ricochet toward the ground after meeting Sixth Batter's bat. Instead, it sails lazily into the air and hovers momentarily above home plate. Catcher positions himself beneath the ball and makes an easy catch for the out. The runner at first base has no choice but to return to the bag. This time, at least, the home team's scouting report has been extremely helpful. With one out, the visiting team is far less likely to attempt a sacrifice bunt. Although the defense must stay prepared, some anxiety has been eliminated.

Starting Pitcher nonchalantly tries to shake some of the soreness out of his elbow as Seventh Batter approaches home plate. Throwing the previous pitch was especially discomforting, and he starts to wonder how much longer he can last. He wants to pitch as long as he can, for he knows he has had more success against the opposing team than have all of the other pitchers. Still, he hopes that the relief pitchers are prepared to enter the day's game earlier than usual.

The first pitch to Seventh Batter is a curveball over the center of the plate, and the batter takes a huge swing. He makes solid contact and hits the ball toward left center-field, but it sails a bit too high to do much good for his team. Center Field is able to make a relatively effortless catch, calling off Left Field long before the ball begins to fall from the sky. The runner at first base did not tag up and is, once again, forced to return to the bag. There are now two outs.

At this point in the game, Catcher demonstrates one of the reasons that he is the team's natural leader. Not only is he the oldest and most experienced player on the team, but he is also the most knowledgeable. Every manager in the league would like to have Catcher on his team. It is a known fact that the veteran spends much of his free time studying the game and other players. During the off-season, he watches videotape of opponents and tries to learn as much about other teams as he possibly can.

Because of his attentiveness to detail through the years, Catcher believes he has learned something about the visiting team's next hitter that probably no other player in the game knows. He has noticed that Eighth Batter usually swings at curveballs only if he must. Even if he knows a curveball is on its way, he will likely pass it up for a fastball unless, of course, he has two strikes and must swing to prevent himself from being called out on three strikes. This isn't always the case, but Catcher believes he has recognized a pattern that might prove to be a weakness for the batter. The veteran recently drew this conclusion after combining his own experience with information gathered while watching a televised game in which Eighth Batter was playing.

Before Starting Pitcher delivers his first pitch to the hitter, Catcher requests a time-out and walks to the mound to inform his teammate of the plan. Starting Pitcher agrees to test the hypothesis, and two pitches later, Eighth Batter finds himself behind in the count: no balls and two strikes. Without even flinching, the batter has watched two slow curveballs cross the plate in front of him. Most players would love to see such perfect pitches, but Eighth Batter is holding out for a fastball. Catcher was right.

With two strikes now on the hitter, Catcher calls for a hard slider on the outside part of the plate. Starting Pitcher agrees, and he, once again, throws the ball exactly as Catcher requests. Because the slider is thrown with much more velocity than the curveball, the spin on the ball is more difficult to see. To Eighth Batter, it appears that the fastball he has wanted is finally speeding toward him. At the last moment, however, the ball drops and slides away from him as he swings and misses, becoming the third out of the inning.

Due in part to the hard work of the researchers who compile information about opposing players, the home team has thwarted the opponent's attempt at a sacrifice bunt. Similarly, Catcher's own knowledge has helped Starting Pitcher to easily retire the last batter of the inning. The special knowledge of a few individuals has benefited the entire team.

———•••———

Acquiring accurate knowledge about opponents has become an important part of the game for all professional baseball teams. In fact, as the years pass, baseball games seem more and more like chess matches. Near the end of close games, dueling managers often find themselves engaged in mental battles that are just as intense as the action on the diamond. When making important decisions, they often rely on statistics and percentages that have been compiled and calculated by other people within the organization. To do what is best for their teams, they must be provided with certain information.

The successful coaches for whom I played kept detailed records about opposing players. One of my former coaches kept charts about the location on the field to which opponents hit the ball and what type of pitches they hit. After recording a few at bats, one could identify certain patterns about the way most batters hit the ball. The vast majority of the time, a hitter will hit the ball to the same general location on the diamond, or he will hit certain pitches to certain places. One of my former coaches always played the percentages, and he was almost always right. I remember a particular game in which an opposing hitter demonstrated a pattern of hitting the ball consistently toward center field. With me at shortstop, my coach signaled for my teammate at second and me to crowd the bag—play unusually close to the middle of the diamond. Consequently, my teammate easily fielded a grounder that would have ordinarily bounced into the outfield. He flipped the ball to me at second base, and the two of us turned a relatively effortless double play. My coach's knowledge paid off.

Today we often see the words *knowledge* and *wisdom* used interchangeably in the Church. Christians have grown accustomed to using the words together and for good reason—the Bible itself contains many passages in which the two concepts are linked. These two words do, however, represent different ideas. And they not only represent different ideas, but according to the Apostle Paul, they also represent two distinct spiritual gifts.

Wisdom, which I believe is a slightly more complex subject than knowledge, will be discussed in Chapter 10. As for the manner in which knowledge was used to further the cause of the early church, it is worth recognizing that knowledge played an important role in reaching tough crowds. A wonderful example is illustrated in Acts 18:24-28:

> *Meanwhile a Jew named Apollos, a native of Alexandria, came to Ephesus. He was a **learned** man, with a thorough **knowledge** of the Scriptures. He had been instructed in the way of the Lord, and he spoke with great fervor and taught about Jesus accurately, though he knew only the baptism of John. He began to speak boldly in the synagogue. When Priscilla and Aquilla heard him, they invited him to their home and explained to him the way of God more adequately.*
>
> *When Apollos wanted to go to Achaia, the brothers encouraged him and wrote to the disciples there to welcome him. On arriving, he was a great help to those who by grace had believed. For he vigorously refuted the Jews in public debate, proving from the Scriptures that Jesus was the Christ* (emphasis added).

The passage above offers a great lesson about knowledge and its relationship to the Body of Christ. In Chapter 1 of this book, I mentioned that Apollos was an important helper to the early church. Because Apollos was knowledgeable, he was able to stand toe to toe with a very intellectual group of people—the Jews—and prove in public that Jesus is the Christ. We can't be certain that Apollos had the so-called gift of knowledge, but we do know that he had a special talent for acquiring knowledge and retaining it. After all, *"he spoke about Jesus accurately, though he knew only the baptism of John.*" The passage does not indicate how much time elapsed between his stay at Priscilla and Aquilla's home and his departure to meet the disciples, but we get the sense that it was not a very long time. And if this is true, it is noteworthy that the "*brothers encouraged him*" to go to Achaia soon after Priscilla and Aquilla "*explained to him the way of God more adequately.*" That is, he learned quickly, and his brothers and sisters in Christ trusted him to be *knowledgeable* enough to face off with the learned Jews and hold his own rhetorically. More important, his knowledge was not used only for his own benefit. He was "*a great help*" to the church at Achaia. His knowledge helped God's team here on earth—the Body of Christ.

CHAPTER 5

Some Prophesy

As the home team takes the field in the top of the third inning, distant rain clouds appear to be creeping toward the stadium. The forecast has promised scattered midafternoon showers, though the amount of rainfall expected is minimal. The ground crew sits watchful and prepared in case a shower should dampen the playing field enough to require their assistance.

Only a few pitches into the inning, the home team finds itself in a bad situation. With the discomfort in his arm worsening, Starting Pitcher is giving everything he has; the team as a whole, on the other hand, is showing a serious lack of focus. First Base has allowed a slow roller to pass between his legs. Second Base has fumbled a grounder, allowing a speedy runner to reach first on what should have been a routine play. Shortstop has misfired a throw into the stands, allowing one run to score; and Center Field has misjudged a fly ball, resulting in two more runs. The home team now trails by three runs. Even worse, there are no outs, and the visiting team has a runner on second base.

Skipper has reluctantly controlled his temper throughout all of the errors, but when Right Field overthrows his cutoff man after a solid hit to the outfield and allows another run to score, the manager feels as if he cannot take anymore. His players are professionals, but they are playing like amateurs. Now trailing 4–0, they are in desperate need of rebuke.

On the rare occasions when his team is playing poorly, Skipper often calls a time-out and walks briskly to the pitcher's mound, where he gathers his infielders and says a few harsh words that are usually followed by a few words of encouragement. The process is called motivation, and being a good motivator is an important aspect of his job. Sometimes, however, for various strategic reasons, Skipper prefers to have Catcher talk to the players.

Skipper has known Catcher for many years. In fact, the two men were actually teammates at one time. Just as Skipper was retiring as a player, Catcher was getting started in the league, and the two of them played one season together. Through the years, Skipper has come to trust Catcher as a valued leader. Players and coaches throughout the league respect the veteran player because of his vast knowledge of the game. Although he is no longer the dangerous hitter that he once was, he is nonetheless an invaluable asset. He is more than a teammate to the other players; he is a mentor. He is the team's unofficial captain, and if Skipper and Coach were ever absent from a contest for any reason, the other players would look to Catcher for guidance. Because he commands such respect, he is often able to motivate his teammates exceptionally well.

Confident that Catcher will speak the words that the other players need to hear, Skipper motions for the veteran to try his hand at leading the team out of a bad situation.

As Catcher tramps toward the center of the infield, he demands that the infielders meet at the mound. As they gather, he shoots looks of disappointment at them one by one. After a few seconds of uncomfortable silence, he says, "What's the problem, fellas? You're playing as if you've already lost the game!"

The other players stare at the ground like beaten dogs. They feel terribly ashamed when they play so poorly that even Catcher chastises them. In his complicated role as a mentor, a respected veteran of the game, and a teammate, he is able to cause self-reflection in the other players that usually leads to their change in attitude.

"We should have already been out of this inning," he continues. "We've made five errors on the last five batters! Concentrate! Skipper is going to be very unpleasant to be around—and we're going to go home with an ugly loss—if we don't get it together soon! Think about what you're doing. We're only behind by four runs. Let's make the easy outs so we can return to offense and score some runs. You're all better than this!"

Catcher glares at the infielders for a few more seconds before turning to walk back to his position. The infielders go their separate ways, knowing that everything Catcher said was correct. They simply need to focus; sometimes they just need to be reminded.

As Catcher settles back into his station behind home plate, Skipper returns to his seat on the bench, knowing that his team captain has perfectly said everything that needed to be said. In a way, Catcher has acted as Skipper's prophet.

In the story, Catcher's gift of prophecy reminds us of the prophecies we read about in the Old Testament. That is, Catcher brings words of rebuke and warning to his teammates. But prophecy isn't always "gloom and doom." In Scripture, prophecy was, quite simply, the will of God or a message from God communicated through man. To be sure, Peter wrote that *"prophecy never had its origin in the will of man, but men spoke from God as they were carried along by the Holy Spirit"* (2 Peter 1:21). In the story, the catcher is the manager's prophet of sorts because he says exactly what the manager wants him to say.

Successful baseball teams usually have one or two players to whom the rest of the team looks for leadership and guidance. I remember one former catcher-teammate who was especially trusted by our coach to say what needed to be said when the team was playing poorly. Big, tough, gruff, and somewhat of a bully, this catcher commanded respect, but not just because of his physicality and attitude. He was also a good player, and he understood the game as intimately as anyone I ever played with. Because he knew the game so well, our coach sometimes looked to him to motivate the team. Our catcher thought like a coach. As a result, he was able to communicate the coach's will.

And by accurately saying what is on the management's minds, players such as the catcher in the story and my former teammate are able to *instruct* the entire team. My former catcher-teammate did not call time-out and walk to the mound just to yell at the other players and me and make us afraid to bump into him on campus the next day. While many of his mid-inning speeches indeed brought rebuke, they also brought effective instruction. He studied opposing hitters carefully and knew well what to do in certain situations. Consequently, he was able to advise us about where to play and what pitches we could expect our pitchers to throw.

The instructional element of prophecy correlates well

with something Paul wrote in his first letter to the Corinthians:

> *Follow the way of love and eagerly desire spiritual gifts, especially the gift of prophecy. For anyone who speaks in a tongue does not speak to men but to God. Indeed, no one understands him; he utters mysteries with his spirit. But everyone who prophesies speaks to men for their strengthening, encouragement, and comfort. He who speaks in a tongue edifies himself, but he who prophesies edifies the church. I would like every one of you to speak in tongues, but I would rather have you prophesy. He who prophesies is greater than one who speaks in tongues, unless he interprets, so that the church may be edified* (1 Corinthians 14:1-5).

Paul expressed the importance of the gift of prophecy because he knew that prophecy edified the church as a whole. Prophecy was an important part of teamwork in the early church.

CHAPTER 6

Some Have Faith

Catcher's forthrightness with his teammates must have had its intended effect, for the home team did not allow any more runs after his visit to the pitcher's mound in the third inning. Moreover, the home team scored four runs in the bottom half of the inning to tie the score of the contest.

In the stands, the fans are excited as ever, happy that their team has rallied to tie the game. Lost has grown quite comfortable talking with Scout, and Scout is finding great joy in sharing stories about his having seen the game of baseball touch many different lives.

To build his own confidence and take his mind off the throbbing in his arm, Starting Pitcher reminds himself that he is the right man for the day's job. Even if his aches and pains affect his pitching so that he is not performing at his best, he is still more acquainted with the opposing hitters than are the other pitchers. His experience alone is invaluable.

His experience, however, does not change the reality that his fastball is losing velocity. On days such as this one—when his arm feels barely capable of pitching a professional baseball game—he is especially thankful that he plays on a team with a fantastic defense. Even though his team-mates on defense sometimes make mistakes, as they did in the previous inning, he knows that they generally commit few errors. He implicitly trusts each fielder who plays behind him. In fact, in a newspaper interview a few days earlier, he acknowledged that his teammates' defensive abilities have been the key to his success throughout the season. He is a successful pitcher because he knows that his arm alone does not win games. More important, Starting Pitcher's faith in his teammates positively affects the entire group. Because the fielders know that he trusts them, they, in turn, play behind him with confidence and a high level of morale.

The visiting team's first hitter in the top of the fourth inning is Ninth Batter. Catcher and Starting Pitcher agree that the first pitch he sees should be a fastball. After a leisurely wind-up, the pitcher delivers the ball to the upper center of the strike zone. Ninth Batter swings hard and connects, but luckily for the home team the ball sails high into the air directly above the pitcher's mound.

It is an unwritten rule in baseball that a pitcher should never attempt to catch a pop-up, even if the ball is hovering immediately above him. This practice has been a part of the game for many years, the idea being that a pitcher should not risk injury if another player can make the catch. So, pitchers must often watch helplessly and have faith that a teammate will come to the rescue.

In the case of Ninth Batter's pop-up, Starting Pitcher naturally takes a few quick steps back while Third Base, Shortstop, and First Base all hustle toward the mound. Third Base, who is the first of the three infielders to position himself beneath the falling sphere, calls off the others.

"I got it! I got it! I got it!"

The others allow him room, and Third Base makes an

easy catch, retiring Ninth Batter for the first out of the inning.

Leadoff, the first hitter in visiting team's lineup, now steps into the batter's box for his third at bat of the game. He senses that Starting Pitcher is wearing down, and he would love to see another of the hurler's fastballs, which are becoming slower and slower with each pitch.

With the pain in his arm now worsening, Starting Pitcher finds himself in an increasingly unpleasant situation. His fastball is no longer very effective, but his curveball causes more pain to his arm. Placing all of his trust in his teammates, he decides to start the batter off with a fastball, and Leadoff, anticipating the type and location of the pitch, smacks the ball down the third-base line.

Third Base quickly moves his glove to his backhand side, and fans cheer in amazement as the fielder snares the well-hit grounder. The cheers turn to gasps, however, as his throw across the diamond leaves his hand on an imperfect trajectory. First Base will have to be at his best to pick the ball from the dirt and retire the runner, who is barreling down the baseline as fast as he can.

"Stay with it, First Base!" encourages Shortstop as he watches the potentially erroneous play unfold.

Third Base's throw is indeed short. The ball bounces four feet in front of First Base, whose concentration, at this moment, is unbreakable. To catch a ball that takes such a bad hop is one of the most difficult plays in baseball.

Starting Pitcher must now have faith again. And he does. First Base is, after all, a professional, and he has made some spectacular plays through the years.

A fraction of a second before Leadoff's left foot comes crashing down onto the bag, First Base secures the badly thrown ball in his mitt.

"Out!" declares the umpire.

Fans applaud in relief, and Starting Pitcher and Third Base both tip their hats to their teammate at first. He has made a difficult play look easy, and the visiting team has two outs.

The next hitter, Second Batter, blasts the pitcher's weakly thrown, three-two fastball in the air down the right-field line. The ball is headed for the corner of the playing field, where, if it lands in fair territory, it will probably result in a double or triple. Starting Pitcher can do nothing but watch and have faith that his teammate in right field will somehow catch the ball before it hits the ground.

As the ball falls from the sky, Right Field races toward the foul line, keeping his eye on the ball as he moves. At the last possible moment, he dives with outstretched limbs and flies horizontal to the ground for a few feet. Just before the ball reaches the earth, it falls into the hustling outfielder's open mitt for the final out of the inning.

Starting Pitcher holds his weathered arm but smiles appreciatively as he jogs off the diamond and into the dugout. He is reminded once again of why he has had so much success. It's good to know people he can trust.

Successful pitchers usually have faith in the defensive abilities of their teammates. After all, not every hitter strikes out. Good pitchers trust that the players behind them can catch and throw and make routine plays. Additionally, pitchers usually learn that the more they express a high level of respect for their teammates, the more their teammates will respect them. When defensive players know that their pitcher trusts them, they are usually all the more eager to perform well behind him.

The year that my high school team won the state championship, we played phenomenal defense. In fact, during the last seven games of the season, we committed only one error—an impressive feat even for professional teams. All of our main pitchers were among the state's top 15 leaders in various statistical categories that year. It wasn't that they all were overpowering; rather, our defense played exceptionally well behind our pitchers. Being one of the hurlers that year, I remember well the confidence I had on the mound. I didn't have to worry about striking out every batter, for I knew that my defense would make the routine plays. They proved their competence again and again. And that experience reminds me of my relationship with God. I trust Him because He's repeatedly proven that He is faithful.

My faith in my teammates also became something from which the entire team benefited. Because I knew my teammates would make plays if the ball were hit, I wasn't afraid to throw strikes. And because I wasn't afraid to throw strikes, I walked very few batters that year.

God's Word contains two examples of how the faith of a small group benefited the whole Body of Christ. In his first letter to the Thessalonians, Paul wrote,

And so you became a model to all the believers in Macedonia and Achaia. The Lord's message rang out from you not only in Macedonia and Achaia— your faith in God has become known everywhere (1 Thessalonians 1:7-8).

By becoming a corporate model for other believers, the Thessalonians would have spiritually edified those in Macedonia and Achaia. After all, to be edified is to grow stronger, and the word *model* implies that the

Thessalonians' faith was something from which others could learn and grow. Furthermore, the gospel message actually spread because of the Thessalonians' faith, for their *"faith in God* [had] *become known everywhere."*

Paul also commended the Thessalonians for their faith in his second letter to them:

> *We ought always to thank God for you, brothers, and rightly so, because your faith is growing more and more, and the love every one of you has for each other is increasing. Therefore, among God's churches we boast about your perseverance and faith in all the persecutions and trials you are enduring* (2 Thessalonians 1:3-4).

In essence, the Thessalonians' faith became a tool by which Paul's messages were strengthened because they brought validity to the very idea of having faith in Jesus Christ. When people remain faithful even during persecutions and trials, others recognize the power of such faith.

Another lesson about faith is found in Paul's first letter to Timothy. Paul gave an instruction to his young disciple that we would all do well to heed:

> *Don't let anyone look down on you because you are young, but set an example for the believers in speech, in life, in love, in faith, and in purity* (1 Timothy 4:12).

Faith was involved in the example that Timothy was to set for others.

Of course, each of these examples deals with the type of faith that all children of God are called to have. As for the actual gift, Paul wrote little, if anything, about it. Many Bible scholars assert that people who have the gift of faith have an extreme confidence in God's ability and willingness to intercede in human activity. Such people place remarkable, and perhaps uncommon trust in God as they go about living their daily lives. In their minds, there is never a hint of doubt that God will provide for their needs and answer their prayers. We have probably all known such people. Their faith is often a beacon of light—an example for all who are watching them and a quality that edifies the entire Body of Christ.

CHAPTER 7

Some Heal

In the top of the fifth inning, the visiting team has come out swinging—and connecting. Third Batter has begun the inning by hitting a double to the warning track, and Fourth Batter and Fifth Batter have both walked. The bases are now loaded with no outs, and Starting Pitcher's already sore arm cannot endure much more. After the base on balls to Fifth Batter, Coach has called a time-out and strolled to the mound to have a talk with his pitcher.

"You're looking a little tired," the coach says to the hurler.

"I'm giving it all I've got, but I don't have much left. My arm just isn't wanting to cooperate."

"How bad is it?"

Hesitantly, Starting Pitcher responds by asking, "Do you want the truth?"

"Enough said," replies Coach. "You've given it your best shot. We'll get Relief Pitcher in to take over from here and see if he can keep those base runners from crossing home plate."

No pitcher likes to leave a game because things aren't going well, but Starting Pitcher takes solace in the fact that his teammate Relief Pitcher is one of the best middle relievers in the game. He is often the medicine of sorts for the starting pitchers. When a starter has a bad day and needs to be delivered from a bad situation, Relief Pitcher is the guy to whom Skipper and Coach look. The starting pitchers trust him immensely because he seldom lets them down. With his hard fastball, vicious slider, and exemplary control, he has "healed," or brought relief to a number of bleak situations during the season. With the bases loaded and no outs, his abilities are desperately needed in the top of the fifth.

As Relief Pitcher makes his way from the bullpen to the pitcher's mound, Coach encourages the infielders and instructs them to try their best to turn a double play if they can get a ground ball. A couple of the infielders tell the tired and aching Staring Pitcher that he has done a good job. And once Relief Pitcher arrives at the mound, Starting Pitcher shares with him important information about certain hitters on the opposing team.

When Starting Pitcher begins to walk toward the dugout, he receives a warm ovation from an appreciative group of fans. Given the pain in his arm, he has performed quite well. And now he hopes to find a more personal type of relief than what Relief Pitcher provided. The hurler has done his job, and he makes his way to the training room, where Trainer will do his own job by icing the pitcher's arm and using his medical expertise to make Starting Pitcher feel better, thereby jump-starting the healing process so that the hurler will be ready to pitch again in just three or four days.

After throwing a few warm-up pitches, Relief Pitcher is ready to face Sixth Batter, who would love to give the new pitcher a powerful greeting by driving in any or all of the runners who are on base.

The new hurler positions himself on the pitcher's plate

and takes his first sign from Catcher. He glances at the runners and then puts all he has behind his first pitch. Sixth Batter simply watches the ball into Catcher's mitt, impressed by the velocity of the pitch.

"Strike one!" announces the umpire.

Relief Pitcher throws the second pitch even faster, and the batter quickly finds he is one strike away from being out.

Then, two pitches later, Sixth Batter goes down swinging at a tricky slider that looked good at first but dropped and curved at the last moment. Finally, the home team has its first out. And Relief Pitcher is one out closer to healing the bad situation.

Seventh Batter is the next of the opposing hitters to be victimized by Relief Pitcher. After the home team's new hurler fools him with two sliders that are called strikes, the now disadvantaged batter is forced to guard the plate. So as not to be called out on strikes, he must swing at any pitch that's even close to being in the strike zone, even if he doesn't like the pitch.

Relief Pitcher delivers a fastball that is an inch or so off the outside part of the plate; however, Seventh Batter must swing just in case the umpire calls the pitch a strike. His swing is weak—more of a protective swing than an aggressive one—and the ball consequently sails lazily into the air on the right side of the infield. First Base makes an easy catch for the second out of the inning.

Watching the game on television from the training room, Starting Pitcher is already feeling better. He appreciates Relief Pitcher's ability to heal the situation on the diamond, and he finds physical relief in the ice pack Trainer has applied to his arm.

Unfortunately, one of Starting Pitcher's teammates will

also soon need Trainer's healing skills and medical expertise.

When Eighth Batter comes to the plate, he hits Relief Pitcher's first pitch solidly into the outfield between Center Field and Left Field. The outfielders hustle to the ball and give their best efforts to make the catch, but in their determination, they collide before either can call off the other. The sound of bones knocking against each other can be heard even over the screaming fans, and both players fall to the grass.

Seeing the collision on the television monitor in his training room, Trainer leaves Starting Pitcher with the ice pack and immediately rushes through the locker-room tunnel and onto the diamond. When he arrives at the scene, he learns that Center Field has already managed to stand and move, with a slight limp, and that he has caught the ball for the third out of the inning.

Trainer's attention now turns to Left Field, who did not fare as well in the collision. Coach, Skipper, and the starting defensive players gather near their fallen teammate, hoping and praying that he is not seriously injured. As the outfielder rolls on the ground in pain, Trainer bends to examine him. Left Field is complaining of a horrible pain in his knee. He is also nauseated. Trainer knows that nausea is usually a sign of a break or severe tear in such a situation, and he consequently knows that Left Field has seen his last play for the afternoon. The player's knee is already beginning to swell, and Trainer immediately applies a dry ice pack to the swelling area and encourages the outfielder to lie still for a while.

Then, after moments of fear and silence from the fans, Left Field rises to the thankful and heartfelt applause of his teammates and thousands of spectators. He will not see any more action for a while, but at least he's up and moving. He is helped off the field and into the training room by Trainer and Coach.

Once inside the training room, Trainer begins to more seriously assess Left Field's injury, knowledgeably asking a series of medical questions and gently feeling the player's knee.

As Starting Pitcher continues to ice his arm, he realizes that the team's two healers—Trainer and Relief Pitcher—are certainly earning their money in the day's contest.

———

I did a lot of pitching during my playing days, and there's one thing I can say for certain about my history as a pitcher: I had plenty of bad outings. I had some good days, too, but even during my best games, my arm was prone to tiredness. I can remember a contest in which I pitched a shutout for six innings, only to lose control and significant velocity in the seventh inning and, consequently, give up seven runs in a period of five minutes. But I also remember that, despite my horrendous seventh inning, my team still won the game. On that occasion, as on many others, I needed a relief pitcher—someone to mend the broken situation I had created by allowing too many batters to become base runners. And on that occasion, as well as on others, the relief pitcher did his job.

I remember how appreciative I was of the teammate who took over for me on the mound and did his job well. A relief pitcher is aptly named, for he indeed brings relief to the previous pitcher and, in fact, the entire team. An effective relief pitcher always gets people's attention. When he brings an end to an offense's successful streak, people notice him and his ability.

Physical relief, or healing, got people's attention in Bible times, too. Healing served as a vehicle for spreading the Word of God and strengthening the Body of Christ as a whole. In the book of Acts we read:

Philip went down to a city in Samaria and proclaimed the Christ there. When the crowds heard Philip and saw the miraculous signs he did, they all paid close attention to what he said. With shrieks evil spirits came out of many, and many paralytics and cripples were healed (Acts 8:5-7).

Some of the miraculous signs to which the passage refers involved the healing of cripples and paralytics. And it was *when* the crowds saw these things that they paid close attention to what Philip said.

Additionally, we know from Jesus' own words that healing helped spread the gospel message. In Matthew we read that Jesus *"called his twelve apostles to him and gave them authority to drive out evil spirits and to heal every disease and sickness"* (Matthew 10:1). What is particularly interesting about this verse is its context. Immediately *before* this passage are Jesus' famous words about the harvest field of souls:

The harvest is plentiful but the workers are few. Ask the Lord of the harvest, therefore, to send out workers into his harvest field (Matthew 9:37-38).

Shortly *after* the verse about Jesus giving the apostles authority to heal, we see that He gave them some specific instructions, saying:

Do not go among the Gentiles or enter any town of the Samaritans. Go rather to the lost sheep of Israel. As you go, preach this message: "The kingdom of heaven is near." Heal the sick, raise the dead, cleanse those who have leprosy, drive out demons. Freely you have received, freely give (Matthew 10:5-8).

It seems that the apostles' powers to heal were directly linked to the message they were to preach on their journey. Many Bible scholars agree that the apostles' healing abilities helped to capture the attention of those who might not otherwise have listened.

A similar lesson can be deduced from the parallel account in Luke's gospel:

When Jesus had called the Twelve together, he gave them power and authority to drive out all demons and to cure diseases, and he sent them out to preach the kingdom of God and to heal the sick. He told them: "Take nothing for the journey—no staff, no bag, no bread, no money, no extra tunic. Whatever house you enter, stay there until you leave that town. If people do not welcome you, shake the dust off your feet when you leave their town, as a testimony against them." So they set out and went from village to village, preaching the gospel and healing people everywhere (Luke 9:1-6).

In both gospel accounts, healing and preaching the kingdom of God seem to be linked. At any rate, Jesus believed it was necessary to give the apostles healing powers before they set out to preach the good news. Obviously, their gifts of healing played an important role in taking the message of Christ to the masses.

Another lesson we can learn from biblical accounts of healing is so obvious that we often forget its importance. To put it simply, healing brought joy. In fact, from Acts 8:8, the verse immediately following the passage about Philip healing and performing miracles in a Samarian city, we learn that *"there was great joy in that city"* because people were being healed.

Furthermore, in the third chapter of Acts, which records Peter's healing of a crippled beggar, we read that the beggar

> *jumped to his feet and began to walk. Then he went with them* [Peter and John] *into the temple courts, walking and jumping, and praising God. When all the people saw him walking and praising God, they recognized him as the same man who used to sit begging at the temple gate called Beautiful, and they were filled with wonder and amazement at what had happened to him* (Acts 3:8-10).

But the healed beggar was not the only one who was so happy that he praised God. According to Acts 4:21-22, *"the people were praising God for what had happened. For the man who was miraculously healed was over forty years old"* (emphasis added). Perhaps some of these people praised God for the first time, convinced of God's power by the healing they had just witnessed.

No matter what one believes about gifts of healing in the twenty-first century, the Bible clearly teaches that healing was used to the same end as all of the other gifts—that is, for the common good of the Body of Christ. It was partly because of healing that the early apostles were able to capture the attention of certain people and, thus, spread the message of the gospel. Furthermore, it brought joy. It was no doubt an important part of the team's work in building up the growing Body of Christ.

CHAPTER 8

Some Perform Miracles

After an impressive display of offense in the bottom of the fifth inning, the home team takes the field with a lead in the top of the sixth. The four runs they scored during their time at bat has put them one run ahead, and the fans could not be happier—even Lost caught himself clapping for the home run that Shortstop hit to make the score 8–7.

Unfortunately, the approaching clouds suggest that rain is imminent. Relief Pitcher has felt a tiny drop of precipitation while throwing his warm-up pitches prior to the start of the inning, and he will probably feel more. Although the rain is not expected to last, it might delay the game for a short time. If so, the ground crew sits prepared to roll the giant tarpaulin back onto the diamond.

In the outfield, Rookie is trying to contain his nervousness about his big-league debut. Due to the youngster's speed, Skipper has chosen Rookie to take the place of the injured Left Field. When Rookie was told he would be seeing action in the game, he started warming up with the anticipation of a child who has just awakened on Christmas morning. And when the home team took the field for defense, he sprinted to his position as though he were in a race. After five years in the minors, his big chance has finally arrived.

Just before play resumes, the announcer addresses the fans to inform them of the new outfielder. After reading some of Rookie's minor-league statistics, the announcer challenges the crowd to warmly welcome the new player to his big-league debut. Obediently, the fans cheer once again and applaud as though Rookie is being welcomed into a new family. Even the vendors and ushers applaud the youngster. Rookie's teammates in the dugout and on the diamond shout encouraging words as well.

After Relief Pitcher has thrown his final warm-up pitch, Ninth Batter comes to the plate determined to start a big inning for his team. Upon seeing the pitch he wants, he swings and hits a deep fly ball down the left-field line. Ninth Batter is a left-handed batter and generally likes to hit the ball toward right field, so the direction of his fly ball has surprised the defense. And Rookie has positioned himself according to the odds, far away from the left-field foul line. As a result, he is now a great distance from the play. The ball looks as if it will land in the corner of the outfield and cause trouble for the home team. Only a miracle will prevent Ninth Batter from reaching base.

The infielders resign themselves to the fact that the batter will probably make it to second and maybe even third. Ninth Batter is, after all, one of the fastest runners on the visiting team. But Rookie is fast, too. In fact, he is so fast that his speed alone has compensated for his mediocrity as a hitter and helped him get to the big leagues. Desperate to impress his manager, the newcomer hustles toward the falling ball with amazing determination and concentration. He glides, as if on wheels, toward the foul line, and in a display of speed that most mortals can only imagine, he reaches with his outstretched arm and makes the catch for the first out of the inning, without even having to stain his uniform. In his big-league debut, his speed has already proven to be an asset for the home team.

Following Rookie's fan-pleasing demonstration of speed, Leadoff connects with a fastball and sends a grounder rolling straight up the middle of the diamond. The ball gets by the lunging Relief Pitcher and bounds at a good pace toward the outfield grass in center field. After it makes its way past the canvas bag at second, it appears as if Leadoff will reach base on a single.

To the spectators' delight, however, Second Base streaks toward the ball and gloves it before it leaves the dirt of the infield. Though his momentum does not allow him to stop, turn, and deliver the ball to First Base as he normally would, he is able to release an accurate throw while off-balance and falling into the outfield turf. Due to not being firmly planted on the ground when he makes the throw, the ball floats toward First Base with just enough kinetic energy to reach its target. Nonetheless, the quickness with which Second Base has fielded and released the ball has compensated for the lack of force behind the throw. Although the play is a close one, the ball reaches First Base's glove in time to retire the batter. Second Base's agility and athleticism have helped him win more than a few defensive awards, and he has once again proven why he is worthy of the honors.

There are two outs when Second Batter digs into the box. He belts a hard ground ball down the third-base line, and Third Base has little time to react. He dives to his right and smothers the ball in his glove to prevent a potential double. He cannot afford to stand and throw to First Base, for doing so would waste precious time as the able-bodied Second Batter sprints down the base path on the other side of the diamond. Instead, Third Base makes the throw while on his knees, using his incredible arm strength to his defensive advantage. The throw is picture perfect, and the runner is out by an entire step. The fans cheer especially hard after this play, for Third Base has earned the reputation of having one of the strongest arms in the league. He is often seen in nightly news highlight films using his strength to throw from a seated or kneeling position.

In the top of the sixth inning, the home team has proven that it can play defense with awesome skill. Rookie's speed, Second Base's agility, and Third Base's uncommon arm strength are almost miracles of nature, and their gifts have served the team well.

Sometimes baseball teams have certain players with God-given talents that amaze us. The abilities to hit home runs, throw 100-mile-per-hour fastballs, or leap high into the air to pull would-be home runs back into the playing area can seem to the average fan like miraculous skills. Spectators enjoy watching such players because their abilities fill us with wonder; managers and coaches like to have such players on their teams because these special talents make their teams better.

As a college player, I had a teammate whose gift of playing third base seemed like a miracle to me. Our diamond was the roughest diamond in the conference, and grounders seldom rolled as players expected them to roll. The area around third base was especially rough. In fact, we scored a lot of runs on visiting teams by hitting the ball down the third-base line. The third basemen for other teams absolutely hated playing on our diamond. Even the best of them seldom had flawless days at our park. Our third baseman, however, had a gift at that position, particularly on our turf. Although the coaches would have preferred to put him at another position, he was the only player on our team who could handle third base on our diamond. But he didn't just *handle* playing third base on our diamond: he played it exceptionally well—so well that other players and coaches often commented about his seemingly miraculous ability to field grounders on such uneven and bumpy ground. His gift certainly benefited the entire team, for we always had an advantage when it came to plays at third base.

Miracles served the early church, too. In the previous chapter we saw that when a group of Samaritans

> *...heard Phillip and saw the miraculous signs he did, they all paid close attention to what he said. With shrieks, evil spirits came out of many, and many paralytics and cripples were healed* (Acts 8:6-7).

This passage suggests that certain instances of healing were miracles. Clearly, though, gifts of healing and gifts of miracles were not always one and the same, for Paul mentioned them as separate gifts.

Still, the ways that these gifts served the early church seem to be almost identical. As we saw in the last chapter, gifts of healing helped to capture the attention of unbelievers. The gift of performing miracles seems to have served the same purpose. To be sure, we should remember a point emphasized in the last chapter: it was *when* the Samaritans saw Phillip's miraculous signs that they paid attention.

A couple of other New Testament passages also suggest that the gift of performing miracles was used to capture people's attention. Paul wrote to the Corinthians that "*signs, wonders and miracles*" are "*things that mark an apostle*" (2 Corinthians 12:12). Applying a little logic tells us that miracles helped apostles convince unbelievers about the truth of the gospel, for the very purpose of being an apostle was to spread the Word of God.

Another important passage about healing is found in Paul's letter to the Romans, in which he wrote of "*leading the Gentiles to obey God by what* [he had] *said and done— by the power of signs and miracles, through the power of the Spirit*" (Romans 15:18-19). According to this verse, miracles did more than simply help in Paul's apostolic endeavor. Indeed, it was *by* the power of miracles that he led the once ignorant Gentiles into obedience to God's Word.

Like gifts of healing, the gift of performing miracles did wonders for strengthening the growing Body of Christ in Paul's time. The general lesson repeated throughout this book applies also to miracles in the early church. God gave gifts to edify the Body of Christ. Each was used to serve the common good.

CHAPTER 9

Some Teach

As the top of the seventh inning begins, rain starts to fall more steadily from the sky. Fans huddle with their families under umbrellas and large sheets of plastic. Not one spectator leaves the stadium, however. Even though the clouds promise a solid shower, the fans dare not miss any action. They are at the park to encourage their favorite players, and encourage them they will.

Since the ball he had used for his warm-up pitches is wet, Relief Pitcher requests a new ball as he climbs the mound to throw the inning's first pitch. Upon receiving the new ball from the home plate umpire, he stations himself atop the pitcher's plate and prepares to throw to one of the best hitter's in the visiting team's starting lineup, Third Batter.

After watching the first two pitches into the catcher's mitt—one, a ball, and one, a strike—Third Batter swings at a hard inside fastball. He hits a grounder into the grass toward third base, and the moisture that has collected on the turf slows the ball immediately. Third Base opens his glove and the ball bounces perfectly into it. It should be an easy play for the fielder.

Although Third Batter is the visiting team's best hitter,

he is one of its slowest runners. He weighs far more than the 230 pounds listed in the program as his weight. He is known for hitting home runs, not for running the bases. Aware of the batter's lack of speed, Third Base takes advantage of the extra time and secures a confident grip on the wet baseball. Confident in his own arm strength, he also takes an extra moment to take good aim at First Base. Because he can throw the ball with such velocity, he seldom has to release the ball as quickly as some of the other players do.

Third Base's close attention to grip and aim fail him, however, as he unleashes a terribly off-target throw. First Base has to remove his foot from the bag in order to catch the ball, and he cannot return to the canvas in time to retire Third Batter. The inning has begun with a home-team error.

Third Base is perplexed. He has one of the strongest arms in the league, but lately he has been making more and more bad throws. Unbeknownst to him, his recent errors have all occurred during the most routine of plays. When he has to dive or rush a throw, he performs flawlessly. Seemingly easy plays, on the other hand, have been ending in errors. All the arm strength in the world means nothing if he can't hit his target. He shakes his head in disbelief and frustration.

Just before Relief Pitcher sets to throw his next pitch, thunder pops loudly overhead and rain begins to fall in sheets. The home plate umpire immediately orders the players off the field and into the dugouts, and the ground crew quickly gets to work on covering the infield with the giant tarpaulin. The rain has arrived, and the game will be delayed until the bad weather passes.

While waiting for the rain to stop, many of the home-team players begin to play silly games in the dugout. One small group starts a friendly but intense game of baseball trivia. Second Base and Center Field politely disagree about who should rightly be called the greatest hitter in the history of the game. The sincere camaraderie is almost tangible. The players truly love working and playing together.

Unfortunately, a couple of the players are not as festive as the others are. Rookie, seated near the bat rack, is discouraged because he struck out in the previous inning. He tries to console himself with the mental reminder that it was his first big-league at bat, but he senses that his offensive abilities are waning. Even his batting practice has been substandard since being called up to the big-league level, and he knows that he is only a mediocre hitter on his best days. He worries that his lack of offensive achievement will force Skipper to send him back down to the minors.

At the other end of the dugout, Third Base wonders why, after years as a professional player, many of his throws to first base are suddenly off target. He is aware of his reputation for being able to throw from unorthodox positions, and he is confident in his arm strength. There must be a basic flaw in his approach to fielding and throwing.

Born with an affinity for underdogs and the downcast, Skipper quickly notices Rookie's pensiveness and takes a seat next to the distraught newcomer. "You're doing well today, kid. You've made a couple of great plays."

Rookie appreciates the encouragement, but he also knows the position he has enjoyed for the past couple of innings is temporary. As soon as Left Field is healed, it is likely that Rookie will once again be watching games from the bench.

"Thanks," he replies weakly. "But why I am having so much trouble hitting the ball? I know I'm not a great hitter, but I was holding my own in the minors. Since coming to this team, even my batting practice has been poor."

Skipper, always prepared to give instruction, seizes the opportunity before him. "You want my opinion?" he asks.

Rookie stops staring at his shoestrings to look up at his manager, somewhat disappointed that Skipper has essentially agreed with the self-assessment. "Sure," he manages.

"First of all," begins the manager, "relax. You're too worried about proving yourself as a big leaguer. You'll get more chances. Second, you're standing too close to the front of the batter's box. Stand as far back as you can, at least for now. Pitchers at this level throw harder than the pitchers you've seen in the minors for the past few years. Stepping back in the batter's box will give you more time to see the pitch and react. A fraction of a second can make all the difference in the world when you're trying to hit a 100-mile-per-hour fastball. And stop trying to hit home runs. You're a rookie; you're not supposed to be an all star yet. In fact, your best asset is your speed. That's why we wanted you to join our team. You can help us a great deal just by hitting singles."

Rookie is amazed by the simplicity of the solutions Skipper has offered. Relax; stand toward the back of the batter's box; don't swing too hard: These are lessons that most players learn in youth league. Still, everything seems difficult when one is having a bad day. Luckily, Skipper has explained things so that they make perfect sense. The manager gives the newcomer an encouraging pat on the back before standing to look for signs of the clouds clearing.

At the other end of the dugout, Coach approaches Third Base and plops himself down beside the reflective infielder. Third Base is staring blankly out onto the diamond, still perplexed as to why many of his most recent throws have been inaccurate. Coach, aware that Third Base is a perfectionist, knows exactly what is going through the meditative player's mind.

"You're thinking about them too long," Coach says matter-of-factly.

Some Teach

"Huh?" replies Third Base, surprised and unaware of Coach's meaning.

"Your throws. You're thinking too hard and long when you field an easy grounder. You know you have a great arm, so you believe you can take a lot of time to aim and think things through before you release the ball. Unfortunately, by taking that little extra time to think, you're making things more difficult than they need to be. Just catch the ball and throw it. The reason you throw so well from your knees is that you don't have time to think about making a mistake.

"You're instincts are some of the best I've ever seen," Coach continues. "Trust them. You've been around the game long enough to know that when negative thoughts creep into your mind, bad things will probably happen. When you field a routine grounder, throw the ball before those thoughts have time to affect you."

Appreciative and aware that his coach is right, Third Base says, "Makes sense."

"Of course it does," Coach replies playfully.

After a few moments, Third Base and Rookie join the fun of the rain delay. Thanks to the insightful teaching of their elders, they can now approach the day with renewed confidence and a more positive attitude.

Following 15 minutes of hard rain, the clouds part and the sun shines brightly onto the diamond. While the ground crew works hard to prepare the field for play once again, the trivia game in the dugout continues, and Second Base and Center Field continue their debate about the best hitter in the history of the game. Shortstop returns to his old friend Scout and visits some more. Lost and his son have gone to the souvenir stand during the rain delay, and Scout tells the shortstop about Lost's dislike of the game. Shortstop, who doesn't like anyone to have a bad perception of the game, takes the information to heart. Perhaps he can do something before the day is over to make the man fond of professional baseball.

A few minutes later, the diamond looks as if no rain has fallen. The tarp has preserved the infield, and the few spots in the outfield and in foul territory that held water have been pumped and raked dry. The umpires declare the delay over, and the players return to their positions.

The home team retires three of the next five batters, allowing no runs to cross the plate. Two of the outs involve Third Base, who twice fields routine grounders and makes perfect throws to first, remembering the advice that Coach has given him.

One of the duties of managers and coaches is to teach their players. Presumably, players at the major-league level need less instruction than do those in the minor leagues, but even the best need to be taught from time to time. There is always something to learn.

In the case of Rookie and Third Base in the story, they do more relearning than learning. That is, they are reminded of fundamental truths about the game and how they should play it. It takes the coach and manager to bring these truths to light, and they do so in a manner that is easy to comprehend. This is one of the true skills of a teacher.

Of course, by analyzing troublesome situations and teaching the solutions to their players, the coach and the manager improve the team as a whole. After Third Base learns what is causing his inaccurate throws, he corrects the problem when he returns to the diamond. He is able to make better throws, and the entire team benefits from his improvement.

In a previous chapter I mentioned that my high school coach was nationally honored for his accomplishments in high school baseball. One of the reasons for his phenomenal success was his teaching ability. I had grown up in a small town that cherished baseball, had played hundreds of games on some of the best teams in the state, and consequently thought I knew all there was to know about the game. When my high school coach arrived at my school, however, he opened up an entirely new world to me because he taught me so many things I did not know. He had a knack for teaching "little things" that many coaches neglect. In fact, he often said, "Offense sells tickets; little things win championships."

And one of the little things he taught me and my teammates indeed turned out to be the most important factor of our championship game the year we won the state title. Until he became my coach, I had always been taught that a pitcher should throw the ball at the batter if the batter attempted a squeeze bunt. The idea behind this squeeze play defense is that the batter will either be so concerned about dodging the ball that he will not even try to bunt it (allowing the catcher to catch the ball and tag the incoming runner), or he will, at best, foul off the pitch and force the base runner to return to third. Even some of my college coaches taught this defense against the squeeze play. My high school coach, however, challenged the logic. His belief was that a batter could still theoretically bunt the ball even if it were flying at his head. So why give him the chance? Instead, he taught the pitchers to throw a pitchout—a pitch so far outside that a batter could not possibly reach the ball. My coach's logic made perfect sense to me.

Not one time during my team's state title season did an opponent attempt a squeeze play—not until the state championship, that is. In the fourth inning of the championship contest, our pitcher had to put into practice what our coach had taught him. Neither team had scored a run, and my team was in trouble. With only one out, the other team had runners at second and third, and their second-best hitter was at the plate. Their coach called a squeeze play, hoping to score a run and gain some momentum—momentum that would have likely broken our backs, as we were already facing the best pitcher in the state. Our pitcher, however, did exactly as he had been taught; he threw the pitch at least a couple of feet outside. The batter did all he could to get his bat on the ball and protect the runner. In fact, he did get his bat on the ball, and the ball flew foul into the backstop. Having to lunge to reach the pitch, though, he stepped on home plate, which is illegal for a batter to do when trying to make contact with a pitch. The umpire called the batter out, and the air was taken out of that team's sails. We retired the next batter, and suddenly *we* had the momentum. We scored two runs in the bottom half of that inning and held the other team scoreless for the remainder of the game.

The state title came down to one seemingly small lesson that our coach was adamant about teaching our team. And he explained the strategy so well the first time we practiced it that neither I, nor any of my teammates, ever doubted it, even though it ran contrary to everything we had previously known about how to defend a squeeze play. His teaching ability definitely benefited the entire team; in a very real way, it helped us win a state championship.

Similarly, Scripture reveals that teaching edified the church as a whole. In his letter to the Ephesians, Paul wrote that, among other types of ministry, God called some to be teachers.

...so that the body of Christ may be built up until we all reach unity in the faith and in the knowledge of the Son of God and become mature, attaining to the

Some Teach

whole measure of the fullness of Christ (Ephesians 4:11-13).

It doesn't get much plainer than that. God called some to be teachers so that the church would be built up. And in his first letter to Timothy, Paul made a similar statement about why he taught. He wrote that God

> *...wants all men to be saved and to come to a knowledge of the truth. For there is one God and one mediator between God and men, the man Christ Jesus, who gave himself as a ransom for all men—the testimony given in its proper time. And for this purpose I was appointed a herald and an apostle—I am telling the truth, I am not lying—and* **teacher** *of the true faith to the Gentiles* (1 Timothy 2:4-7 emphasis added)

The *purpose* for which Paul was appointed to be a teacher was to communicate with the world that God wants all men to be saved. God wants His team to be as big and strong as possible, and by teaching about Jesus Christ, Paul strengthened the greatest team of all.

Teaching helps us grow stronger in Christ. Quite simply, sound teaching makes us better. And as the interaction between Coach and Third Base in the story illustrates, even when teaching is done on an individual basis, the learner can strengthen a team or a group with his newfound knowledge. Third Base strengthened the team when he stopped making errors during routine plays. Similarly, a single Christian can strengthen the entire Body of Christ when he or she has been taught something new. As Paul wrote to the Corinthians, the Body is made up of many parts (1 Corinthians 12:12). And what affects one part affects the whole.

67

CHAPTER 10

Some Have Wisdom and Some Have Discernment

The home team left the bases loaded in the bottom of the seventh inning, so the score is still 8–7 as the top of the eighth begins. The visiting team could tie the game with one swing of the bat, and its best batters will soon come to the plate. The contest is still far from over. The home team must stay focused and not become complacent.

Ninth Batter leads off the inning for the visiting team. He swings at Relief Pitcher's first offering and hits a high pop fly into foul territory by the third-base dugout. Although the play should be Third Base's to make, Shortstop hustles to get beneath the falling ball just in case Third Base loses it in the sun or stumbles. And it's a good thing that Shortstop is there to back up his teammate, for Third Base indeed stumbles. He snags one of his spikes on the giant tarpaulin and, consequently, loses his chance at making the catch. Shortstop, attentive to the situation, reaches into the seats as far as he can, and the ball falls into his mitt for the first out.

As fate would have it, Shortstop's mitt is almost laying in Lost's lap as he makes the catch. Immediately remembering what Scout told him about Lost's dislike of the game, Shortstop seizes an opportunity to win over a new fan. Although the ball would normally go back to the pitcher after such a play, Shortstop gives it to Lost's son—the second ball he has given the child during the course of the afternoon. Lost is surprised and touched by the player's generosity and attentiveness to his son.

Shortstop also takes the time to make a comment to Lost. He doesn't want the man to leave the park unaffected, and he wants to make the most of the opportunity before him. Before returning to his position, he thanks the man and his son for not interfering with the play, as so many fans do when a foul ball falls in the first row of seating. Lost, of course, would never dream of interfering with a play, but he is impressed by Shortstop's cordiality. He now sees that not all professional players are egoists who don't appreciate fans. Shortstop seems to be a genuinely nice guy. He returns to his position feeling good about the few seconds he has taken to interact with Lost and the boy. He made the most of a seemingly small opportunity.

As Leadoff strolls slowly and confidently to home plate, Visiting Manager makes an unexpected move. Although Second Batter is due to bat after Leadoff, the manager tells him to remain seated. Instead, he directs his best, but presently injured hitter, Deception, to get a bat and move to the on-deck circle. Deception is one of the league's best hitters, but due to a severe leg injury, he has not played for many weeks.

Visiting Manager's plan is simple. He knows Second Batter has an unsuccessful history against Relief Pitcher. Deception, however, is one of the few players in the league who has consistently done well against the pitcher. If Leadoff were to reach base, he would represent the potential tying run for the visiting team, and Deception would be the right hitter to produce a hit that might score the runner. Visiting Manager knows that Skipper is aware of Deception's success against Relief Pitcher, and Visiting Manager would like to lure Skipper into replacing the talented pitcher.

In reality, however, Visiting Manager has no intention of sending Deception into the game. The skilled player has been recuperating from his injury for a long time, and his absence from the starting lineup has cost the visiting team dearly. He has nearly recovered and is almost ready to reclaim his position, but close to being fit is not good enough in professional baseball. For Visiting Manager to send him into a game now—so close to the end of his full rehabilitation—would simply be too risky. His appearance in the on-deck circle does draw a lot of attention, however, and that is the precise effect that Visiting Manager had hoped for. When one of the league's best hitters has been sitting on the bench for weeks and then suddenly emerges from the dugout to the on-deck circle late in a close game, everyone begins to murmur.

Skipper simply takes note of the situation and begins to think it over carefully.

Before Leadoff steps into the batter's box, he stops to take a few practice swings. He seems to make a show of swinging extraordinarily hard, and he slowly scans the outfield wall with his eyes, as if looking for the best place to hit the ball over the outfielders' heads.

When Leadoff finally steps into the batter's box, Third Base notices something peculiar about the hitter. Leadoff has positioned himself as far forward in the box as is legal.

Always attentive, Third Base quickly processes the batter's cunning plan. In hopes that the infielders will position themselves toward the back of the infield, Leadoff has attempted to make the home team believe that he will swing for the fence. If Third Base is far enough away from home plate, Leadoff can execute a surprise bunt down the baseline and reach first easily.

However, the batter has underestimated Third Base's eye for detail. Third Base knows that a bunt is likely when a batter, especially a fast runner such as Leadoff, takes his stance toward the front of the box. Standing toward the front of the box makes certain pitches easier to bunt. It also places the batter a few inches closer to first base, and a few inches can sometimes be the difference between being safe and out. In addition, Leadoff poses a threat as a bunter anyway. Besides being fast, he bats left-handed, which naturally gives him an additional one-step advantage in sprinting to first, since the left-handed batter's box is slightly closer to the base than the right-hander's box.

As Relief Pitcher takes the sign for his first pitch to Leadoff, Third Base stands deep in the infield, close to the arc where the outfield grass meets the infield turf. He wants to appear as if he has been fooled. But just before the pitch leaves Relief Pitcher's hand, Third Base sprints toward home plate.

Determined not to give away his own plan, Leadoff keeps his hands in the swinging position for as long as he can. But in the end, he indeed squares to bunt.

Relief Pitcher has thrown him an outside fastball, which is a good pitch for a left-hander to bunt down the third-base line. The batter gently taps the ball with his bat, and the ball begins to roll slowly toward the base.

If Third Base had been fooled, the bunt would be a good one. The fielder's attentiveness and discernment, however, have allowed him plenty of time to make the play. He fields the ball cleanly and makes a perfect throw to First Base.

The play is not even a close one. The field umpire declares Leadoff out, and the frustrated runner shakes his head in amazement, wondering how Third Base could have possibly known of his intentions.

Now there are two outs in the top of the eighth. The players and the fans wait for the talented Deception to take his position in the batter's box. The match-up between the batter and Relief Pitcher is a legendary one. Almost every fan in the stadium knows that during his career, Relief Pitcher has given up more home runs to Deception than to any other opponent, and a home run now would tie the game. Deception takes his time with a few more practice swings in the on-deck circle, and Visiting Manager waits as long as he can to call him back to the dugout. The manager is hoping that Skipper will call a time-out, walk to the mound, and substitute another pitcher.

But Skipper doesn't call a time-out, and he doesn't walk to the mound. He simply shouts a few encouraging words to Relief Pitcher and his other players, urging them to keep playing good defense. He has called the other manager's bluff.

When the home plate umpire begins to appear impatient, Visiting Manager sends Second Batter to home plate and orders Deception to return to the dugout.

Second Batter, who has only one career hit in more than 30 tries against Relief Pitcher, strikes out on three pitches.

Skipper's discernment has helped him win a mental battle with the opposing manager. When Skipper thought hard about the situation, he knew Deception's trip to the on-deck circle was a bluff. He knew that the hitter had not warmed up at all before the game. Given Deception's injury, Visiting Manager would have informed his star player before the game if there were any possibility that he might play in the day's contest. Surely, Skipper thought, Deception would have done minimal pre-game stretching exercises if Visiting Manager were seriously considering such a move. In addition, Skipper knows how much money the visiting team has invested in Deception. To risk further injury could be costly in more than one way.

Skipper doesn't always like the fact that his job requires him to make difficult decisions, but he's glad he has the mental capacity to lead his team. His players are glad, too. His discernment, as well as that of Third Base, has benefited the entire team in the eighth inning.

And as Lost begins to probe Scout for more information about Shortstop, Scout thinks of how wise it was of Shortstop to make the most of a chance opportunity to further goodwill and better the game's reputation with a fan. One more fan can only make the team a little bit stronger.

———

Although my high school team finished as state runners-up my senior year, we did not have a great offense. In fact, at most, we had three good hitters, and we seldom scored a lot of runs. Consequently, our coach had to be a very wise offensive strategist and take advantage of every opportunity to score. And he was wise, indeed. Since most of us were not exceptional hitters, our coach called for a lot of bunts, steals, and hit-and-run plays. We might not have scored many runs, but we didn't leave many runners on base either. We took advantage of our opportunities, in large part because of our coach's wise decisions.

In the story, Shortstop also demonstrates the ability to take advantage of an opportunity. Though it wasn't necessary, he fosters more goodwill with Lost and the boy after catching a foul ball near their seats. It was wise of the shortstop to take the time to speak with Lost and give the child another souvenir. Winning over one more fan can only strengthen the team as a whole.

You might be wondering why I have alluded to making the most of opportunities in this particular chapter. The reason is simple: According to Scripture, making the most of an opportunity is an element of wisdom. The Apostle Paul wrote two almost identical instructions about wisdom and opportunity. He instructed the Ephesians to live *"not as unwise but as wise, making the most of every opportunity"* (Ephesians 5:15). And to the Colossians he wrote, *"Be wise in the way you act toward outsiders: make the most of every opportunity"* (Colossians 4:5).

These two verses teach us that wisdom is an ingredient of recognizing the potentiality of a situation or occasion. Interactions with outsiders provide varying degrees of opportunity, and the fruit produced from those opportunities may vary depending on the amount of wisdom employed in those situations. Any fruit that does come from such interaction is good for the Body of Christ as a whole, for when an outsider is positively affected by the witness of a believer, God's kingdom scores a victory. Just as the shortstop in the story tries to score a victory for the home team by winning the respect of a new spectator, or an outsider, Paul instructed early Christians to be wise in their interactions with nonbelievers. And to make the most of every opportunity was to demonstrate the love of Christ in a way that would cause outsiders to see that love in the believers.

Scripture also relates wisdom to discernment, or what the *New International Version* of the Bible terms *"distinguishing between spirits"* (1 Corinthians 12:10). The author of Proverbs wrote:

Wisdom will save you from the ways of wicked

men, from men whose thoughts are perverse, who leave the straight paths to walk in dark ways, who delight in doing wrong and rejoice in the perverseness of evil, whose paths are crooked and who are devious in their ways (Proverbs 2:12-15).

The book of Proverbs also says that wisdom will protect us (4:6). So what does this have to do with discernment? Paul wrote a great deal about false prophets, and it was because of false prophets that the gift of discernment, or distinguishing between spirits, was even needed. The spirits between which certain Christians distinguished were of two types: godly and ungodly. Logic tells us that the ungodly spirits were of men with evil intentions, and according to Proverbs, wisdom is a protection against such men. In short, wisdom and discernment are closely related in Scripture.

Just as players and managers use trickery and deceit in baseball, the enemy has tried again and again to attack the church through falsehood. Paul wrote to the Romans:

I urge you, brothers, to watch out for those who cause divisions and put obstacles in your way that are contrary to the teaching you have learned. Keep away from them. For such people are not serving our Lord Christ, but their own appetites. By smooth talk and flattery they deceive the minds of naive people. Everyone has heard about your obedience, so I am full of joy over you; but I want you to be wise about what is good, and innocent about what is evil (Romans 16:17-19).

Paul was instructing the Romans to stay away from deceivers altogether. And part of the protection against deception included being wise about good things. Moreover, the passage teaches that such wisdom was good for the church as a whole, for the people who taught false doctrines caused divisions in the body.

One of my college coaches had an amazing ability to call the right defensive plays when our defense was faced with runners at first and third. First-and-third situations are advantageous for offenses because they allow so many productive possibilities and, consequently, keep defensive coaches and managers guessing. The coach to whom I refer, however, had a gift. He almost always knew exactly what the offense would try to do, and consequently he was able to instruct his infielders to make plays that often thwarted the offense's efforts. Whether it was to align for a double play up the middle or to rotate a certain way on a bunt, he always seemed to know what to do in every situation. I don't know how he knew; he just did. He could anticipate the opposing team's trickery and make decisions that were good for our team.

Just as baseball teams need players and managers who can recognize trickery in certain situations, Paul informed the church that it needed people who could distinguish between spirits. After all, he told the Corinthians, "*Satan himself masquerades as an angel of light. It is not surprising, then, if his servants masquerade as servants of righteousness*" (2 Corinthians 11:14-15). Luckily, God provided a gift for recognizing such deception and keeping the team strong and united.

CHAPTER 11

Some Administrate

The home team scored four runs in the bottom of the eighth inning, making the score 12–7. Two players blasted home runs, and the visiting team committed two errors, which took the wind out of their sails. The fans thoroughly enjoyed the inning; now they are ready for the home team to get the last three outs so they can finally claim victory.

Skipper has made a couple of important end-of-game managerial decisions, substituting players at two positions. First, he has chosen to replace Relief Pitcher with Closer. Closer is a tall, hard-throwing right-hander who often pitches in the final inning. Because he throws so hard and expends so much energy with each pitch, he can perform at his best for only a few outs. But the velocity of his fastball makes him incredibly difficult to hit. Hence, he is the pitcher who closes games in which the home team has a lead as it heads into the final inning. Closer is the best finishing pitcher in the league, and he's had four days of rest, so he should be ready to throw extremely hard. Given that Relief Pitcher was beginning to show signs of fatigue and Closer is so well rested, Skipper thought the change to be a wise administrative decision. Relief Pitcher understands that the move is a good one for the team, and he is proud to relinquish control of the mound to such a fine teammate.

Skipper has also made a change in the outfield. Right Field is an exceptional hitter, and he has one of the strongest throwing arms in the game. However, he is a large man who is not a very fast runner. Since the home team has a five-run lead and most likely will not have to bat again, Skipper thought it would be a good idea to replace Right Field with a faster player and narrow the chance of the visiting team gaining last-inning momentum by getting any extra-base hits. Skipper has chosen to replace Right Field with Utility because Utility has the foot speed to reach fly balls that might elude the starting right fielder.

When Third Batter comes to the plate to try to begin something big for the visiting team, he feels the effects of Skipper's wise administrative decision to bring Closer into the game. Closer's first pitch is faster than any pitch the hitter has seen in a long time. He simply watches it into Catcher's glove and awaits the umpire's declaration of "Strike!" Third Batter prepares himself as well as possible for the second pitch but manages only to hit a weak foul ball. Within seconds, the hitter finds himself with two strikes.

Two pitches later, Third Batter returns to his seat in the dugout, unsuccessful against the new hurler. He has become just another statistic in Closer's professional file of strike outs.

As Fourth Batter, the visiting team's most powerful hitter, makes his way to the batter's box, the visiting team begins to make rally noise from the dugout. The intention of such noise, continuous and chaotic encouragement, is to increase Fourth Batter's adrenaline and create mental havoc for the other team. But the noise from the visiting team's dugout can be only faintly heard, for the home-team fans, excited about being only two outs away from victory, are making a lot of noise of their own and trumping the efforts of the visiting team.

To the disappointment of his teammates, Fourth Batter does not fare any better than Third Batter. Although he manages to foul tip a tricky slider, Closer's fastball proves to be too much for the hitter in the end. Fourth Batter also strikes out. The home team is now one out away from victory.

As Fifth Batter takes his stance in the batter's box, almost all the spectators in the stadium rise to their feet to applaud and shout. An incredible amount of noise reverberates throughout the park, giving the home-team players a burst of adrenaline. The team has put on a great show for its supporters, and the appreciative fans are now eager to share in the joy of victory.

The players for the visiting team have all but given up. Falling behind by five runs has weakened their resolve, and they know that, with only one out to spare, their chances of achieving a come-back victory are now slim at best.

Closer's first pitch to Fifth Batter is a hard fastball over the center of the plate. The hitter manages to make contact, and the ball sails deep into right field, which is now being patrolled by Utility. The new outfielder immediately turns and hustles toward the wall. His first step on the warning track lands him precisely where a puddle of water had formed during the rain shower. If not for the excellent work of the ground crew, he would slip and fall. Fortunately, the area is now dry and his momentum continues to carry him back. Just before crashing into the wall, he collects the ball with his mitt and squeezes it tightly. Utility slams hard into the padded barrier but manages to hold on to the ball as his body absorbs the shock of the collision.

Although he is slightly jarred, he rebounds with a festive

smile. At last, the final out has been made, and the home team can declare victory. Utility jubilantly tosses the ball into the stadium seats as a souvenir for one of the fans, and Skipper takes comfort in knowing he made the right administrative decision by replacing Right Field with Utility. Because he is a slower runner, Right Field simply would not have made the catch.

The home-team players gather near the pitcher's mound to congratulate one another on a well-played game. And as photographers and news reporters swarm the infield, trying to obtain interviews with some of the players, thousands of loyal fans applaud and cheer all at once. Young and old alike beam with pride, grateful that their support has not been in vain. When the players win, the fans win, too. And even Lost, to his child's amazement, stands and sincerely applauds for the home team.

After the happy fans start to file out of the stadium, Boss begins to find his way from his skybox to his team's locker room. One of the reasons he is so respected as an organizational leader is that he is sensitive enough to encourage his players on a regular basis. He often steps briefly into the locker room to thank the players for their hard work. He even says a few kind words after tough losses. The players appreciate his habit of remembering them. And his kindness makes them a better team, for the nicer he is to them the more they want to honor him with hard play and victories.

On his way down to the showers, Boss even stops to speak with food and souvenir vendors. He knows most of them by name, and he remembers the names of many of their children and spouses. It is by understanding the importance of humility, kindness, and encouragement that Boss has been deemed one of the best administrators of the decade.

Just outside the locker room, he must weave his way

through a maze of reporters, guards, and privileged fans. Of course, reporters approach him for interviews, and he is always happy to give them, but he does so only after he has spoken to his players.

Once he is inside, he says a few kind words to individual players, laughing and congratulating each on certain accomplishments during the game. When the noise quiets enough for his voice to be heard by everyone, he says simply, "You guys did a great job today. Good luck tomorrow." And that's all. He hasn't said much—only ten words—yet to the players these words mean a great deal. Everyone likes to be appreciated.

On his way out the door, he quietly discusses some business with Skipper. He informs the manager of his administrative decision to have an autograph session prior to the next evening's game. Because of a few reckless players throughout the league, the game has received some unfavorable media attention during the past few weeks. Boss would like his players to do something nice for their fans and help counter the bad publicity the game is getting. Like Shortstop and Scout, he knows that strengthening the reputation of the game in general can only strengthen the team. After sharing his idea with Skipper, he faces the reporters, being polite and patient with them.

A few moments later Skipper calls his team together for a post-game talk. He is happy about the outcome of the game, and he tells his players so, but he is not satisfied with the team's overall performance. Although they have played well, they have still made a few mistakes.

"First of all," he begins, "good job. You guys didn't give up when the game was close, and then you scored four runs in the last inning to give us an easy win. You did a lot of things right today. Most of you hit the ball well, and some of you made some incredibly fine plays in the field.

"However, we still have some things to work on. Coach, read the stats that you and I were discussing a few minutes ago."

Coach, leaning against the outside of a shower, begins to read from a notebook. "Six errors—most of them in one inning. Nine strikeouts. Nine runners left on base."

"We have to eliminate the errors," Skipper continues. "They add up. And we have to score runners when we get them on base. In the third inning, we had the bases loaded with no outs, and we failed to score; there's no excuse for that. You're a great ball club, but you have to stay focused every minute of the game. Other teams always know when you're losing focus, and they will take advantage of your mistakes.

"But to get back to the positive stuff, there is one thing that I especially want to commend you for today: You did a great job of working together as a team, just as you have all season. Everyone in this locker room contributed to today's victory. You all knew exactly what your roles were, and you were all happy to do your part to help the team. That's what teamwork is all about. When you all make efficient use of your individual abilities and use those abilities in harmony with everyone else's, you are unbeatable."

The players are filled with a warm sense of pride, for it is the love of teamwork and camaraderie that keeps them playing the game.

"Now," continues Skipper, "we have one more home game before leaving for a five-day road trip. There are a couple of things we need to work on, so be here at 9:00 tomorrow morning for a short practice. Then I want *everyone* to arrive at the stadium at least three hours early for tomorrow night's game. Boss wants to do something nice for our most dedicated fans, and he has asked that you sign autographs for the early arrivers. We have some of the greatest fans in the game, and I agree with Boss that we should show our appreciation. Moreover, because of a handful of careless players in the league and reporters who don't like your success, both you and the game have taken some knocks in the press lately, and every player has an obligation to represent it as well as he can. Every player has an obligation to represent the truth."

The players agree, for they have all been victimized by unfavorable media coverage that has made all players out to be just alike—greedy and reckless and indifferent to fans' feelings. No matter how fan-friendly players are, some people will always belittle and mock them, but they will nonetheless keep doing their part to serve the game.

Skipper has once again proved worthy of the respect he is given throughout the league. His administrative skill in the final inning helped the entire team. Closer was able to prevent any runners from reaching base, and Utility made a play that the starting right fielder could not have made, possibly thwarting a rally by the visiting team.

Boss has also made a wise administrative decision. He hopes to foster goodwill through autograph signing the next evening. He appreciates the fans, and he knows that showing his appreciation can only strengthen the organization as a whole.

Wise administration benefits the common good.

One of the college teams I played on had three catchers who brought different strengths and weaknesses to the team. Two of them were exceptional defensive players with strong arms but were only average hitters. The other was clearly the best hitter of the three, but he wasn't as strong on defense. It was difficult to assess who the best all-around catcher was.

Because all three of the catchers worked hard in practice, our coach decided to give them each approximately equal playing time. But he did not simply rotate them every third game, nor did he choose the starting catcher on a whim. He made his decision about which catcher would start depending on a number of factors: the team we were playing, the nature of the opposing pitcher, and the nature of our own starting pitcher. Each game our coach thought carefully about which catcher would be best for the team, and the circumstances of the moment determined his decision. By assessing the situation and choosing his catcher accordingly, our coach was being a wise administrator.

When we think of administration, we often think of someone telling others what to do. But there's more to administration than giving orders. A good administrator has a gift for seeing the big picture and knowing how to arrange the various parts for the good of the whole. The manager in the story made wise administrative decisions when he replaced the relief pitcher and right fielder with players whose abilities could better serve the team in the final inning.

In the book of Acts, Luke recorded a wonderful example of wise administration:

> *In those days when the number of disciples was increasing, the Grecian Jews among them complained against the Hebraic Jews because their widows were being overlooked in the daily distribution of food. So the Twelve gathered all the disciples together and said, "It would not be right for us to neglect the ministry of the word of God in order to*

*wait on tables. Brothers, choose seven men from
among you who are known to be full of the Spirit
and wisdom. We will turn this responsibility over to
them and will give our attention to prayer and the
ministry of the word."
This proposal pleased the whole group. They
chose Stephen, a man full of faith and of the Holy
Spirit; also Philip, Procorus, Nicanor, Timon,
Parmenas, and Nicolas from Antioch, a convert to
Judaism. They presented these men to the apostles,
who prayed and laid their hands on them.
So the word of God spread. The number of disciples in Jerusalem increased rapidly, and a large
number of priests became obedient to the faith* (Acts
6:1-7).

There is an important administrative lesson in this passage. The 12 apostles did not rush in to take care of the
widows themselves. It wasn't that they lacked love or compassion for them; rather, they simply thought about the
greater good before acting. They knew that their most important job was prayer and ministry of the Word, so they
needed others to care for the widows. In short, they dele-
gated because that's what was best for the Body of Christ as
a whole. And the word *so* at the end of the passage indicates
that it was *because* of the apostles' wise administration that
"the word of God spread " (v. 7). The apostles adminis-
trated wisely.

The Bible does not use the title *administrator* to refer to
church leaders. However, I believe that the titles *elder, over-
seer,* and *pastor* refer to those who made administrative decisions. And while I do not believe that one necessarily had
to be a church leader in order to perform administrative

tasks, I do believe that all church leaders were administrators in some regard. Paul wrote of elders "*who direct the affairs of the church*" (1 Timothy 5:17), and Peter wrote that elders were to be "*shepherds of God's flock*" (1 Peter 5:2). The word *shepherd* implies some decision-making responsibility.

And if we can make the connection between church leaders and administrators, then we can see that Paul gave some clear instruction about the necessary characteristics of administrators. Paul told Timothy and Titus that overseers were to be, among other things, above reproach, temperate, self-controlled, respectable, hospitable, able to teach, able to manage, and of good repute (1 Timothy 3:2-7; Titus 1:6-9). Throughout the story contained in this book, the home team's manager, coach, and owner demonstrate such qualities and thus find favor with their people. The manager and coach have reputations as being two of the game's wisest and best studies, and they are, of course, able to teach and manage. Similarly, the team's owner has a great reputation as an employer. He is also able to manage, and he is hospitable in the way he treats his employees.

So how do these qualities in administrators benefit the entire team? The answer is a common sense one. No one wants to be under the influence of administrators who are mean, insensitive, and disrespectful. Bad administrators break up teams. Good administrators help keep them together by showing genuine concern for the various team members.

CHAPTER 12

Each One Is a Part of the Team

During the course of the afternoon, the man named Lost has been genuinely impressed by the decency of Scout and the home-team players, especially Shortstop. The star infielder has been more than simply cordial; he has gone out of his way to brighten a child's day by retrieving and autographing a baseball. Furthermore, he has treated Lost with kindness and respect. Shortstop's gift of being an ambassador for the game has had a profound impact on the man who detested professional baseball only a few hours earlier. As Lost begins to look for his car in the parking lot, he is almost sad that he has to go home.

As if by fate, Lost sees a familiar face when he finds his car and begins to unlock its doors. Parked directly next to him is Scout. Unknowingly, a smile comes across Lost's face. There is something about Scout that is genuine and honest, and Lost is glad that they have bumped into each other.

After exchanging a few kind words, Scout mentions that he has not learned Lost's last name. Always an ambassador for the organization, the talent seeker looks at the child and says, "I want to be able to recognize this little guy's name on the sports page some day."

The boy swells with pride, and Lost pats his son on the head as he replies, "Nowfound. My last name is Nowfound. And I hope to see you again at the park some day. I think I'll bring my son to every Sunday home game."

"That would be wonderful," Scout replies. "The organization appreciates all the fans it can get."

As usual, Scout will drive away from the stadium with a sense of satisfaction that goes beyond his love for baseball. He loves his job mostly because it affords him opportunities to spread goodwill, and he is always amazed at how easy it is to affect someone's life with stories about the game. Today the ambassador has affected more than just a single life: he has helped bring a father and son closer together.

After most of the fans and players have left the stadium and driven away, Boss finishes some business in his office and begins to make his way toward the parking lot. Walking past the clubhouse, he notices that Skipper and Coach are still working, discussing the day's game and making administrative decisions about the next evening's contest. Boss is thankful that he has a manager who is such a good leader. Skipper's administrative abilities, both on and off the diamond, are respected throughout the league.

As Boss continues through the lower part of the stadium, he looks through a tunnel to the diamond and sees that the ground crew is still working on the field. He also sees vendors and ushers helping to pick up trash around the seats. A smile crosses his face as he takes satisfaction in the fact that so many of his employees selflessly help the organization by doing so many thankless jobs. Not only do the vendors and ushers help in a number of ways during the game, they also help long after most people have gone home. Boss then thinks back to before the game started, when even some of the players, such as Rookie, Bullpen Catcher, Utility, and other nonstarters gave generously of themselves to help the starting players warm up.

Boss realizes, too, that helping is only one piece of the organizational puzzle. His organization runs smoothly and his team is successful because everyone contributes to the betterment of the whole. Boss pauses as he remembers various moments of the day's game: Rookie's display of almost miraculous speed; Second Base's and Third Base's seemingly miraculous defensive plays; Relief Pitcher's ability to heal a broken situation left behind by the tired Starting Pitcher; Trainer's expertise in handling Left Field's unfortunate injury. Thanks in part to Trainer's skills, Left Field will recover, and Starting Pitcher will be ready to pitch again in just a few days. Everyone has a purpose.

Boss also realizes that the players and other members of the organization use their gifts, talents, and abilities in ways that he and most people will never know about, for not all contributions are visible. Very few people in the stadium knew that Third Base's discernment prevented Leadoff from reaching base on a tricky bunt. Only Skipper, Coach, and Visiting Manager know that Skipper's discernment helped him win a mental battle with the other manager in the eighth inning.

Only Scout knows of the wisdom that Shortstop used when he made the most of an opportunity and went out of his way to be cordial to a man who was cynical about the game and its players. Neither Boss nor the thousands of fans were aware that Coach and Skipper used their superb teaching ability to help Third Base and Rookie overcome problems in their game. Only Starting Pitcher fully appreciates how having faith in his teammates' defensive skills helped him make it through the first few innings with his troubled arm. Catcher's gift of prophecy—his ability to speak for the manager and motivate the team—will never be mentioned on the evening news, nor will his detailed knowledge of opposing hitters and the way that knowledge helped Starting Pitcher to strike out Eighth Batter in the second inning. The organization's statisticians and various people who obtain knowledge about the other players in the league will likely never be lavished with praise either. Only the home-team fielders fully appreciate how Second Base and Shortstop interpret the catcher's signals and cunningly alert the defense to what pitches are being thrown, allowing the defense to make plays it might not ordinarily make.

And only Lost and his grateful son will remember how Shortstop and Scout served as wonderful ambassadors for the game and the team, dispelling Lost's negative perception of professional baseball and its players.

Boss knows nothing of these things. He only knows that everyone has an important job to do, and he's glad to be in charge of an organization in which team members—all of them—accept their roles and use their abilities for the greater good.

In the last two or three decades, *teamwork* has become somewhat of a buzzword in our society. School curriculums now emphasize collaborative work, and businesses and corporations spend thousands of dollars on teamwork training. Unfortunately, the Body of Christ has not paid as much attention to the subject—which is too bad, since God's Word provides a lot of instruction about teamwork.

First Corinthians 12 is rich with instruction about teamwork in the church. While the chapter has traditionally been labeled the spiritual gifts chapter, I've come to call it the teamwork chapter. I realize the passage is about spiritual gifts, too, and I certainly don't want to minimize the importance of spiritual gifts in those verses. However, as the passage indicates, gifts are manifestations—actions through us—of the Holy Spirit. When we have gifts, we have to *use* them.

More importantly, we need to use our gifts as a team. Partly because of the *help* of others, Paul was able to accomplish great things as an *apostle*. The *teaching* of some helped provide others with a great deal of *knowledge*. The *administrators* of the early church needed *wisdom* and needed to surround themselves with wise people. Without *faith*, no *tongues*, *interpretations*, *healings*, or other *miracles* would have occurred. The list could go on and on. The early church prospered, in part, because the believers used their gifts together.

In a very real way, Paul was writing about teamwork in 1 Corinthians Chapter 12. And Paul's use of the human body to illustrate what teamwork should look like in the Body of Christ provides us with some wonderful lessons. Some of the most important are listed below.

1. TEAMWORK IS THE OTHER PART OF UNITY.

What do I mean by "the other part"? Many times Christians think about mental unity or doctrinal unity when they think about unity within the Church. You've probably heard 1 Corinthians 1:10 quoted in discussions or sermons about unity. Paul wrote,

> *I appeal to you, brothers, in the name of our Lord Jesus Christ, that all of you agree with one another so that there may be no divisions among you and that you may be perfectly united in mind and thought.*

Another popular verse about unity is found in Philippians 2:2, in which Paul wrote, *"...make my joy complete by being like-minded...."* Many Christians tend to think of agreement when they think about unity.

Obviously, mental or doctrinal agreement is important, but there's another aspect to unity. There's more to Philippians 2:2: *"...make my joy complete by being like-minded, having the same love, being one in spirit and **purpose"*** (emphasis added). According to Paul, unity involves not only agreement but also action.

If you bend down to pick something up off the floor, all of your body parts do some work. Your eyes guide your fingers, your toes help you to balance, and your hands lift the object. In essence, your parts are working as a team. If the parts are not unified in action, picking something up off the floor becomes a difficult task. As Paul's illustrative use of the human body demonstrates, teamwork is a part of unity.

2. TEAMWORK IS A PART OF MEMBERSHIP AND THEREFORE EVERYONE'S BUSINESS.

In 1 Corinthians 12:24, Paul wrote that *"God has combined the **members** of the body"* (emphasis added). He also told the Corinthians that they were *all* members of the Body of Christ: *"Now you are the Body of Christ, and **each one of you is a part of it"*** (1 Corinthians 12:27 emphasis added). Paul's allusion to membership can teach us a lot about teamwork. Almost daily, I receive mail offers to become a member of some group or organization, and in order to be a member, I must do something. If I am to become a member of a book club, I have to buy books. I will enjoy certain benefits because of my membership in that book club, but I will also have to act—with my checkbook.

When you bend down to pick something up off the floor,

the members of your body must do work. Why? Because they all belong to the body. When we eat, the various parts of our bodies benefit from the nutrients we absorb, but they also contribute to getting those nutrients into our bodies. It's not just our mouths that do the work. Our legs and feet get us to the table, our hands and arms help us get the food to our mouths, and our hearts pump blood so that those parts can do what they need to do.

Teamwork is a part of membership; therefore, it's everyone's business.

3. TEAMWORK SHOULD BE INCREDIBLY EFFICIENT.

When you need to pick an object up from the floor, you don't stand on your head and try to lift it with your toes. Your gift of administration—your brain—knows that it's most efficient to bend at the knees and waist, balance with your legs and feet, and pick up the object with your hands and fingers. As Paul's analogy of the human body demonstrates, true teamwork should be incredibly efficient.

4. TEAMWORK SOMETIMES INVOLVES CARRYING EACH OTHER'S BURDENS.

"The eye cannot say to the hand, 'I don't need you!' And the head cannot say to the feet, 'I don't need you!'" (1 Corinthians 12:21) The believers in Corinth were trying to "one up" each other with the use of their spiritual gifts. Some in the Corinthian church thought they were better or more important parts of the body because they had certain gifts, and other people's gifts were viewed as less desirable. That's why Paul wrote the words above.

But the verse has another implication. Suppose again that you need to bend down and retrieve something from the floor. Now suppose you don't have the use of your eyes.

How are you going to pick something up off the floor if you can't use your eyes? If you've ever watched a blind person, you know the answer. Blind people use other senses, particularly the senses of hearing and touch, to compensate for their lack of sight. If you were blind and dropped something on the floor, you would feel around until you found it.

Sometimes certain parts get broken or tired in the Body of Christ. That's when other members of the body have to carry extra weight. The eye cannot say to the other parts, "I don't need you."

5. TEAMWORK CAN INVOLVE BOTH DISTINCT AND OVERLAPPING ROLES.

I'm glad that I have two hands, ten fingers, ten toes, but only one nose. I would look funny with two or three noses. Some of the parts on our bodies are duplicate parts that perform similar or identical tasks. Some parts are distinct and have distinct purposes.

Sometimes in the Body of Christ, especially in smaller churches, people feel as though they have to bring new and different gifts to the congregation. And it's great when they can, but it may be perfectly fine if a lot of people have similar gifts and talents. Sometimes jealousy even creeps into the church because some Christians don't want other Christians to have the same gift that they have. However, repeated throughout 1 Corinthians 12 (verses 6, 11, 18, 24, 28) is the idea that God Himself has arranged the parts of the body. If we truly trust in God and the direction of His Holy Spirit, we'll understand that some people's roles in the Body of Christ will be unique, while some people will have the same gifts and abilities that others have.

6. TEAMWORK INVOLVES HAVING EQUAL CONCERN FOR EACH OTHER.

Paul wrote that the parts of the body *"should have equal concern for each other"* (1 Corinthians 12:25). Pretend for a moment that a criminal approaches you on the street and tries to punch you in the face. Instinctively, you will raise your hands and arms in protection, covering your face and head as well as you can. Now pretend that the criminal tries to punch you in the stomach. Your hands and arms will instinctively try to protect your midsection. The hands and arms have equal concern for the different parts of the body. They don't protect the face and ignore the stomach. If one part gets hurt, the whole body feels the pain.

7. TEAMWORK IN THE BODY OF CHRIST REQUIRES INTIMACY.

This is the most important rule and the one that ties all of the others together. Paul wrote in verse 26 of 1 Corinthians Chapter 12, *"If one part suffers, every part suffers with it; if one part is honored, every part rejoices with it."* People cannot genuinely rejoice and suffer with one another unless they are intimate.

For example, I have a friend who loves God and America's pastime. He would love to be a chaplain in professional baseball. Assume for a moment that he were going to be honored with that job. The person who would rejoice the most for my friend would be his wife, for no one is more intimate with my friend than she is. She would know more than anyone how that honor had fulfilled a deep desire in his heart and brought him inexpressible joy.

Now, assume my friend attends church the Sunday after he has received the good news about his new job. The pastor, who is happy for my friend, announces the news to the congregation. Some of the churchgoers shake my friend's hand after church; others get in their cars and drive away without saying a word to him. It's not that my friend's church family doesn't love him. Rather, the degree to which the members are intimate with him determines the degree to which they rejoice with him. Those who know him best will shake his hand and maybe give him a hug. Other people in the congregation will not even say, "Congratulations." However, God's Word does not say, "Those of you who are close to each other should rejoice and mourn together." Paul gave the directive to the entire church. The implication is that each individual church body should be as intimate as possible.

When a person's hip or knee is dislocated, we might say that the knee or hip, literally speaking, is not as intimate as it's supposed to be with certain parts of the body. Consequently, the body doesn't work properly. Teamwork in the Body of Christ requires intimacy.

Teamwork is a fundamental part of God's plan for humanity. In fact, it was one of His first gifts to humankind, for according to Genesis 2:18, *"The Lord God said, 'It is not good for the man to be alone. I will make a helper suitable for him.'"* In other words, God blessed Adam with Eve because Adam needed help. The first man could not handle everything himself.

As a divinely given gift for service, I believe that Christians should try to incorporate the concept of teamwork into their lives more deliberately and more often. Through 1 Corinthians 12, God has provided us with a paradigm for what teamwork should look like in the Body of Christ. He has also provided us with abundant evidence of how certain gifts and characteristics edified the early church. Recognizing that evidence should encourage us because it is more proof that God's Word is true and that He is faithful in all of His promises. If we use our gifts in the right way, God will use us to edify the Body of Christ. We can enrich other people's lives as well as our own by using the teamwork paradigm of 1 Corinthians 12. Moreover, using God's model of teamwork can help us serve Him more efficiently and more effectively.

There are different kinds of gifts, but the same Spirit. There are different kinds of service, but the same Lord. There are different kinds of working, but the same God works all of them in men.

Now to each one the manifestation of the Spirit is given for the common good. To one there is given through the Spirit the message of wisdom, to another the message of knowledge by means of the same Spirit, to another faith by the same Spirit, to another gifts of healing by that one Spirit, to another miraculous powers, to another prophecy, to another distinguishing between spirits, to another speaking in different kinds of tongues, and to still another the interpretation of tongues. All these are the work of one and the same Spirit, and he gives them to each one, just as he determines.

The body is a unit, though it is made up of many parts; and though all its parts are many, they form one body. So it is with Christ. For we were all baptized by one Spirit, into one body—whether Jews or Greeks, slave or free—and we were all given the one Spirit to drink.

Now the body is not made up of one part but of

many. If the foot should say, "Because I am not a hand, I do not belong to the body," it would not for that reason cease to be part of the body. And if the ear should say, "Because I am not an eye, I do not belong to the body," it would not for that reason cease to be part of the body. If the whole body were an eye, where would the sense of hearing be? If the whole body were an ear, where would the sense of smell be? But in fact God has arranged the parts in the body, every one of them, just as he wanted them to be. If they were all one part, where would the body be? As it is, there are many parts, but one body.

The eye cannot say to the hand, "I don't need you!" And the head cannot say to the feet, "I don't need you!" On the contrary, those parts of the body that seem to be weaker are indispensable, and the parts that we think are less honorable we treat with special honor. And the parts that are unpresentable are treated with modesty, while our presentable parts need no special treatment. But God has combined the members of the body and has given greater honor to the parts that lacked it, so that there should be no division in the body, but that its parts should have equal concern for each other. If one part suffers, every part suffers with it; if one part is honored, every part rejoices with it.

Now you are the Body of Christ, and each one of you is a part of it. And in the church God has appointed first of all apostles, second prophets, third teachers, then workers of miracles, also those having gifts of healing, those able to help others, those with gifts of administration, and those speaking in different kinds of tongues. Are all apostles? Are all prophets? Are all teachers? Do all work miracles? Do all have gifts of healing? Do all speak in tongues? Do all interpret? But eagerly desire the greater gifts (1 Corinthians 12:4-31).

ABOUT THE AUTHOR

Gentry Sutton is the founder of Diamond Ministry, through which he shares "biblical truth about teamwork to enrich the Body of Christ and the culture." He holds bachelor's and master's degrees in English, and he and his wife Brooke have two sons and a daughter.

For more information about Gentry and his teamwork ministry, visit www.diamondministry.com.